ALSO BY P. M. FORNI

Choosing Civility: The Twenty-five Rules of Considerate Conduct

THE
CIVILITY
SOLUTION

THE CIVILITY SOLUTION

WHAT TO DO WHEN PEOPLE ARE RUDE

P. M. FORNI

Founder of The Civility Initiative at Johns Hopkins

ST. MARTIN'S GRIFFIN
NEW YORK

www.stmartins.com

The Library of Congress has catalogued the hardcover edition as follows:

Forni, P. M.
    The civility solution : what to do when people are rude / P. M. Forni.
        p. cm.
    ISBN 978-0-312-36849-4
    1. Courtesy. 2. Etiquette. I. Title.
    BJ1533.C9F67 2008
    395—dc22

                                                                    2008009448

ISBN 978-0-312-36964-4 (pbk.)

First St. Martin's Griffin Edition: September 2009

10   9   8   7   6   5   4   3   2   1

To Virginia, always

Debts of Gratitude

This book was made possible by the willingness of acquaintances, friends, and family to share their encounters with rudeness. At Johns Hopkins the focus group assembled by my good friend Macie Hall included Cheryl Wagner, Mark Cyzyk, and Reid Sczerba. The participants in the Towson group were Bill Leeb, John Colmers, Marci Treece, James Bailey, Crystal Guerngerich, and Debby Viles. There are many others, in both Italy and the United States, who I hope will forgive me if their names do not appear here.

Over the years I have accumulated a great debt of gratitude to David Stevens and Treva Stack of the Jacob France Institute at the University of Baltimore. Still in Baltimore, Warren Green and Ian McFarlane, the very civil leaders of LifeBridge Health and EA Engineering, Science, and Technology, never fail to help when I knock at their corporate doors. I owe thanks to Dr. Rudolph Hoehn-Saric and Dr. Stephen Reich, outstanding physicians and advocates of civility. My student assistants and my whole department at Johns Hopkins University have facilitated my work year after year. Once again, I am happy to acknowledge the support of the university's president, Dr. William Brody.

My gratitude also goes to my good friends Dr. Arthur Ciaramicoli and Dan Buccino. They were very generous with their time as they checked the accuracy of the manuscript's psychological parts. In Spokane, Christie Toribara of SMILE (Students Mastering Important

Lifeskill Education) helped with the section on bullying. Robin Dellobough, a gifted professional reader, helped by balancing and polishing the whole text. Cordial thanks go to my agent, Lisa Di-Mona, for doing things right one more time. At St. Martin's Press, Vice President George Witte and my editor, Michael Flamini, believed in the concept right away and provided support, insight, and professional wisdom. Vicki Lame was an asset that made the difference.

I owe my greatest debt of gratitude to my wife, Virginia. Among the many forms her boundless love can take is tough and enlightened criticism. Without her steering of the early drafts in the right direction, I would have spent a lot of time and energy with little to show for it. This is as much her book as it is mine. I love you, Ginnerella.

Versions of small sections of this book appeared in *Johns Hopkins* magazine, *The Journal of Employee Assistance,* and *Clinician News*.

Contents

A List of the Situations
Presented in Part Two

THE NEIGHBORS—NOISY, NOSY, AND NICE   103

WORKPLACE WOES   112

ON THE ROAD, IN THE AIR, AND
ABOARD THE TRAIN   126

Preface

IF ANYTHING CHARACTERIZES THE TWENTY-FIRST CENTURY, IT'S
OUR INABILITY TO RESTRAIN OURSELVES FOR THE BENEFIT OF
OTHER PEOPLE.

—*James Katz*

This is how Marci recalls the one encounter with rudeness that sticks in her mind:

"Needing to run a quick errand before work, I threw on a business suit and ran out the door. Driving north on a wide through street, I climbed a small hill to a stoplight. A man in another car was waiting for me to pass so he could pull out of his subdivision. I did pass and then stopped at the red light a few yards up to make a left turn. The man pulled up alongside me to turn right at the light and leaned out of his window. The nasty expletive exploded from his lips. It was pure spite delivered with shocking bluntness. At least the kids weren't in the car to hear him. Shaken, I began to tremble—not with anger but with the sting of an unexpected wound.

"Why me? Why such an extreme reaction? Didn't he see I was just a working mom, driving my minivan to work? I wasn't ignorant or inconsiderate, selfish or dim-witted, and I certainly was not what he called me! The unfairness of it all hit me. Should I follow this man and at the first opportunity demand an explanation?

Maybe offer an apology? No, better to do my errand and get to work. I began to cry.

"I felt so abused, so punished, so violated, so deeply hurt, and eventually very angry that I could not defend myself. The incident affected me for days afterward. The next time I climbed that hill to the stoplight, I looked around to see what I might have done to cause the outburst. Eventually, after a long time, I realized it was more the man's problem than mine."

Marci's tale is unusual only because she never did find out what caused the stranger's outburst. Her emotions, however, are quite familiar. All of us have been shocked by people behaving rudely. Rude relatives, bosses, co-workers, "fellow" drivers, and strangers in literally all circumstances of life have made us feel at fault, helpless, and angry. We have bristled at the unfairness of their attacks and at times endured lingering hurt. Clearly a problem in the lives of individuals (with negative effects not only for its victims but also for its perpetrators), rudeness is also a social problem with costs estimated in the billions of dollars.

Rudeness may be everybody's everyday problem, but millions remain unprepared for their encounters with it. This book aims to help you find exactly what rudeness is and how it works. Most important, you will learn how to defend yourself effectively and civilly from its daily challenges. Being civil is the sterling strategy for rudeness prevention. If you are respectful and considerate, most of the people with whom you come in contact will be motivated to be the same in return. When rudeness can't be prevented, civility is still your best choice, as the stories that follow show over and over again.

Although we cannot hope to ban rudeness from our lives altogether, we can limit both its occurrences and its impact. When we handle it well, we feel good about ourselves and reap other substantial benefits, such as healing wounded relationships. Being prepared is half the solution to any problem. Put this book to work for you, and never let rudeness catch you unprepared again.

Precisely because rudeness is quite common, it is not a trivial issue. Indeed, in our day-to-day lives it is possibly responsible for more pain than any other mortal failing.

—Emrys Westacott

Our ability to deal with rudeness is somehow related to how we handle grief, and the series of steps that we go through in coping: shock, denial, anger, acceptance, and finally release. Of course the narrative for a loss occurs over a protracted period of time, while the rude encounter's narrative is far shorter.

—James Bailey

PART ONE

Wisdom and Skills

1. On Rudeness

Eight tough weeks into my stint as a reluctant conscript in the Italian Army, I was not looking forward to another ten months in the stark isolation of my remote Alpine outpost. I knew I would miss civilian freedom and the excitement of city life. Newly licensed to drive military trucks, I could see in my future only long and bleary-eyed shifts steering diesel behemoths along treacherous mountain roads. Then, one cold December morning, everything changed. Transfer orders came, like an extravagant early Christmas gift. I was to report to brigade's headquarters that very evening. My C.O. informed me that I would be in charge of a new military newsletter and act as liaison with the local press. The brigade was headquartered south of the mountains in a lovely town graced by elegant Renaissance buildings, filled with art treasures, and swarming with life. Congenial work awaited me. Relative freedom came with the job. I felt as though I was rejoining civilization, and I was moved by my own good fortune. Still incredulous, I packed my few belongings, put on my travel uniform, and arranged a ride to the train station.

As the train pulled away from the frozen wilderness, my heart soared. The sky had loomed overcast since morning, but as we left the last of the shaded gorges and uncoiled onto the flatland, the afternoon sunshine made its glorious appearance. While the golden light raced us down the rust-colored countryside, I became sharply aware of a rush of happiness inside me. I was simply, perfectly happy. And with that happiness came the determination to always remember how it felt. There was no assurance that I would ever experience it again. I wanted to remember the electrical warmth of the train compartment, the smell of the vinyl upholstery, the preternatural quality of the light, the surge inside. Everything. The way the world felt the moment I was happy.

Moments like this make life worth living. They are rare and usually come out of the blue. We are visited by them just as the ancients were visited by their gods. This does not mean, however, that in the realm of the ordinary there is no room for happiness. It may be a happiness of a different kind, but it too makes our days worth living. When you are asked if you had a good day, what allows you to answer that you did? Not that you experienced rapturous joy but rather that a few defining—albeit mundane—good things happened to you. You may think, for instance:

"I really got a lot done at work today. The office finally came together as a team, without the usual power games and personality clashes. The Big Boss even acknowledged that my marketing plan was very smart. Is a promotion next? Salad with Jennifer at lunch was a treat. We must do that more often. She took it in stride that I had to remain at work late again tonight and said she would be glad to pick up the children at school. I will make it up to her. I am so lucky to have her in my life. The drive home was no struggle, for a change. No tailgating, no angry honking, no wild lane hopping. People were in a wonderful merge-and-let-merge mood. No stress there; in fact, some friendly waving. Wouldn't it be wonderful if it was always like that?"

You may not have experienced a single "brilliant flash of enjoyment" (to use John Stuart Mill's expression), but you are *happy with what you did, happy with your day*. You feel good about yourself and about the world. This ordinary happiness, this feeling of contentment can become your faithful companion. It's the state of mind you refer to when you say that you are *happy with your life*. What you mean is that you are gratified by a number of good things that are part of your daily experience. How is life treating you? That depends to a large extent on how *others* are treating you and how *you* are treating them. In the preceding example, the events forming the good day all involved people relating positively to one another.

Unfortunately, as a society we seem to be failing the respect-and-consideration test. Opinion surveys have been reporting for years that Americans are quite concerned about the incivility they encounter every day. They feel they have been witnessing a steady decline of standards in their lifetimes and see no realistic indication that a trend reversal is around the corner. A detailed picture of incivility in the U.S. today will emerge from the following pages and chapters. Suffice it to say, for now, that the threat of incivility to the quality of our lives is not a trivial one. Common sense suggests that we should learn to cope as best we can with the rudeness that will certainly keep coming our way. To do that we need to acquire clear notions of what rudeness is, what it does, and what causes it.

WHAT IS RUDENESS?

AS A COURTESY TO THE
NEXT PASSENGER MAY
WE SUGGEST YOU USE
YOUR TOWEL TO WIPE
OFF THE WASHBASIN

Have you ever noticed this kind of sign in an airplane restroom? I find it truly extraordinary. It is the voice of society reminding us that we are expected to care for one another. We are *expected,* mind you, not *required.* The sign makes no reference to a law or even a regulation. The key words are "as a courtesy" and "we suggest"—nothing more than a gentle prodding. But why should we clean out a basin that a perfect stranger will use next? Why spend time and energy on something that does not benefit us directly? Because it is *the right thing to do.* Being courteous to the next passenger is its own reward, the sole incentive. A remarkable notion!

Several decades ago, Sir John Fletcher Moulton, a distinguished British judge, spoke of a sphere of human action he called Obedience to the Unenforceable. Actions in this realm are neither prescribed by law nor chosen in absolute freedom. Rather, they are influenced by our sense of what is the proper, responsible, and decent thing to do. They fall under an unofficial code of duty to goodness. If we fail to yield our subway seat to a frail and aging fellow passenger, the law will not come after us. And yet, something makes us forgo our comfort. We are free to remain seated, yet we are not *completely* free. Civility compels us—at least some of us—to stand.

When we obey the Unenforceable and clean up after ourselves in an airplane restroom, in addition to being courteous to the next passenger, we keep alive an unwritten pact that benefits us as well. It is a pact with no one in particular and with persons of civil disposition in general, based on the principle of reciprocal altruism. If each passenger is willing to do his or her part, the basin will always be clean for everybody. It is an efficient and even enlightened system in which self-interest and altruism harmoniously converge. But it is also a vulnerable one, and its downfall is rudeness, one definition of which is "taking without giving." The rude disregard the Unenforceable. They enjoy the clean basin but neglect to clean it in turn. They flout the rules of civility while counting on others to follow them.

RUDENESS DEFINED

When we are polite, we confer regard. The original meaning of *to regard* is "to look," "to notice," and "to keep in view." To *dis*regard, then, is to look elsewhere, to withdraw attention—and, with it, respect and consideration. Rudeness is *dis*regard. It diminishes and demeans. By treating others curtly, we put them in their place, which is a way of controlling them and thwarting their attempts at controlling us. Through rudeness we show off, dominate, intimidate, coerce, threaten, humiliate, dissuade, and dismiss. Rudeness is control through invalidation. Acts of rudeness can ruin our days and sometimes remain etched in our memory for years. They come in many varieties, but they have one thing in common: They bruise and wound. This is the reason rudeness warrants the investment of time and energy necessary to understand it and learn effective ways of dealing with it.

UNFOCUSED RUDENESS

Suppose your friend and co-worker Matt says he's going to invite you to lunch to meet someone he thinks could help you in your work. Then Matt invites someone else instead. He is not targeting you in particular for rude treatment—he just found it more convenient to change plans. He also skips his four o'clock appointment with another colleague and permanently forgets to return several phone calls. That's how he functions: He is rude to the world. Although some people might label Matt's behavior lack of consideration, I call it "unfocused rudeness." Those indulging in this kind of disregard let doors swing into other people's faces, play loud music late at night, march into crowded elevators before anyone can get off, and litter without remorse. They may even put their booted feet on your brand-new sofa while decrying today's civility decline, but they do so in a haze of obliviousness rather than out of deliberate choice. They are rude to you because you happen to be around.

You can always choose to ignore unfocused rudeness. If you are inconvenienced by it, if it hurts your feelings, or if it puts you in an awkward position, by all means speak up. Doing so will make it less likely that you have to deal with such slights again. In the case of the business lunch that never materialized, you can say to Matt: "You know, when you invited me to have lunch with you and Dr. Powell, I cleared my calendar for the whole week to make sure I could. I thought you meant what you said. I didn't expect that you would just not call." Unfocused rudeness is generic and mindless, and it does not bear the sting of hostility. But it is still rudeness, and it can disrupt and annoy, as the two following examples show.

A librarian notices that one of the computers available to the library's patrons has been unplugged. A young woman is sitting at the working computer next to it. "Have you been using this computer?" the librarian asks, pointing to the disabled one. "No," she says, "I turned it off because it was making noise." "You disabled a computer that others might need?" asks the librarian. The young woman shrugs. "It was making noise. I didn't feel like listening to it." The librarian turns the computer on and says, "Please, don't turn it off again." Sadly, she is very much used to seeing her patrons choose the course of action that is easiest for them without much regard for the needs of others.

The famous author arrives at the bookstore thirty-five minutes late for her reading. Quick to blame bad traffic, she does not men-

UNFOCUSED RUDENESS WITH CELL PHONES

An enormous amount of unfocused rudeness is generated by the use of cell phones in public places. Not only is the inconsiderate handling of cellular communication annoying for those exposed to this form of noise pollution but cellular rudeness can also be disruptive of the client–service provider encounter. The Spokane pharmacist Christie Toribara deals every day with clients who expect to conduct their business with her while on the phone with someone else. "It is quite an effort," she says, "to gather the needed information from clients, including spelling of name, address, phone number, allergies, and insurance, to proceed with the filling of a prescription. The problem presents itself again when clients pick up their prescriptions. Most states require medication counseling for the clients' safety. When they are engrossed in conversation on the cell phone, my clients miss or don't understand important points. Often they will not step back to let others be helped, thus slowing things down for everybody else. This is a waste of time for the the pharmacist, who cannot dispense the medications until the counseling is completed. It would be a simple courtesy toward others and the professional staff to turn off or not answer cell phones when seeking help at a pharmacy."

tion bad planning on her part. Is she happy finally to greet the local loyal and curious, some of whom have waited for an hour or more to see and hear her? Not quite. She informs her audience that this is the last stop on an exhausting cross-country book tour, and you know how wretched those things are. (None of the aspiring writers in the room *do* know, but of course they would like to with all of their souls.) So there she is, expected to summarize her novel's plot as she has done so many times in the last four weeks. "I'm starting to hate the damned thing," she says half-seriously. By the way, has anyone here noticed that her book's title was taken from the Bible? No? Well, never mind. They didn't at her readings in San Diego and Cleveland either. Actually, she says, biblical allusions are all through the book, but people just don't get them. By now some members of the audience resent being portrayed as sorry ignoramuses standing between her and her rest and relaxation. They would welcome a few gracious words, but she appears totally unaware of her audience's feelings, her common sense no match for her narcissism.

FOCUSED RUDENESS

Suppose, now, that rather than simple lack of consideration, your colleague Matt's reneging on his invitation is part of a power game intended to affirm his dominance. This would be *focused* rudeness. Focused rude people will keep interrupting you, hoping to impress the boss, ask you embarrassing questions in front of your co-workers, gossip maliciously about your private life, and even race you to the coffee machine for the last cup to avoid making a new pot. When you and your actions or accomplishments do not conform to their wishes, they respond aggressively. Focused rudeness is often caused by anger and is mean-spirited. An act of focused rudeness can leave you feeling violated and feeling vulnerable to being controlled by the other person.

Sometimes blatant and sometimes stealthy, focused rudeness does more serious damage than the unfocused kind. The first thing to do when coping with an act of rudeness is to assess quickly whether it is focused or unfocused. Determining which will help you decide what to do. Has Matt "forgotten" to invite you because he envies your achievements? If so, is he likely to hurt you again? In what ways? You may still decide not to do anything for the moment, except file

PORTRAIT OF FOCUSED RUDENESS

Virginia still remembers being the victim of mean-spirited focused rudeness many years ago. Proud of her brand-new, spotlessly white canvas sneakers, she hoped that they would forever keep their bright, clean look. She knew they wouldn't, but they were still in mint condition, and throughout the day she couldn't help but occasionally glance at them, smiling inside. She felt silly—a small thing like a pair of sneakers giving her such pleasure—but who cared? She wore them to a barbecue party that evening. The patio was crowded, beer flowing, the smell of grease in the air, the floor littered with fallen food. Beer bottle in hand, an old friend from high school asked her if she was having a good time, and she said yes. Then he noticed her sneakers. "Brand-new sneaks, eh?" he said, grinning. "They need to be broken in." He stepped on one of her shoes, rubbing his dirty sole on the white canvas, and then stepped on the other as well. Virginia stared at the smeared sneakers and at him, aghast and feeling violated.

the incident away in your mind for future reflection and action. If you are detecting a pattern of bias against you, consider making an appointment with Matt to discuss the issue. A good alternative is to speak with a supervisor. Continued focused rudeness can qualify as bullying or harassment.

THE OFFENSIVE ANCHOVIES

There are rude people (plenty), and there are people who can be rude (virtually everybody else). In other words, there are both habitual and occasional offenders. And both kinds can engage in both focused and unfocused rudeness. The combination that we witness more often is unfocused and occasional. Incidents of this kind are also more likely to have satisfactory resolutions. Here's an example from my own life.

One night, after ordering my usual margherita pizza at a restaurant near home, I said to Allison, my very young waitress: "And please, add a few anchovies." She made an exaggerated expression of distaste, exclaimed, "We don't have anchovies—they are disgusting! They would stink up the whole place if we had them," and left. Although a little taken aback, I was not indignant. Allison's reaction *was* rude, but there was certainly more innocence than malice in it. It was incomprehensible to her that anyone would be so foolish as to order something so foul. Maybe she thought that I needed to be dissuaded from committing the same mistake in the future.

After she left to place my anchovy-free order, I decided that I owed it to both myself and her to say something. When she came back asking if everything was to my liking, I said that it was. Then I added, "Would you mind if I gave you a suggestion about work? Don't tell a customer that something he likes is disgusting. It doesn't make him feel good and makes you sound unprofessional." Allison's response was heartening: "You know, I thought of that and wondered, maybe I should not have said it. It's just that I really dislike anchovies. I apologize."

Inexperience and spontaneity tripped her up, but this was a minor and occasional lapse on the part of a considerate young woman. I accepted the apology and in turn said I hoped I had not hurt her feelings. She assured me that I had not and was most cordial when she brought me my check. I felt good about having spoken, I felt good about her reaction, and I felt good about the achieved closure. A venial act of rudeness had produced a cathartic and warm outcome.

WHAT DOES RUDENESS DO?

How does rudeness damage us? By causing stress, eroding self-esteem, creating problems in relationships, making things difficult at work, and escalating into violence.

It Adds to Stress

First of all, rudeness is a stressor and can have a negative impact on our health. Following an exchange of rude remarks, anger-laced words fly between Toby and Alex. Cascades of catecholamines, the stress response hormones and neurotransmitters, flood their brains and bloodstreams. This activation of their bodies' emergency systems is not without a price. Neurochemicals such as epinephrine, norepinephrine, and cortisol increase blood pressure, sometimes to dangerously high levels. They affect the metabolism of cholesterol and triglycerides, which contribute to atherosclerosis. Known to weaken the immune system, they block the activity of the macrophages (killers of tumor cells). Although one catecholamine-laden altercation will not destroy Toby or Alex, repeated engagements of their stress response will add substantially to the wear and tear on their organs and blood vessels. If they frequently find themselves in the grip of hostility and anger, they may sooner or later face serious cardiovascular disease and other ailments. Becoming skilled at preventing rudeness and responding to it limits the damage that stress inflicts upon body and mind.

It Erodes Self-Esteem

Rudeness wears down our mental defenses, leaving us vulnerable to self-doubt and anxiety. An overweight woman hears the anonymous message on her voice mail that the circus is looking for a fat lady. In the middle school cafeteria, a clique of girlfriends moves to another table when an undesirable outsider sits near them. For no apparent reason, a supervisor fails to elicit one employee's input, and when she volunteers it, he disregards it. These victims of rudeness and hostility may respond with resentment and even anger. The feeling that they deserve the abuse, that they must be somehow defective or inadequate, may be part of their response as well. People can withdraw or become aggressive as rudeness diminishes their self-esteem. Either way, their relationships with co-workers, friends, and family suffer—a damage that takes a further toll on their sense of self.

It Is Bad for All Kinds of Relationships

We are hardwired to relate and connect. During the course of our lives, we involve ourselves in innumerable relationships of all kinds. Common interests, intellectual and physical attraction, and the sheer human need for company are just a few of the scores of incentives to enter and remain in relationships. So we try to keep our relationships alive, and when they end, we often experience feelings of failure and loss. Healthy relationships remain so and survive in part thanks to the relational skills of the partners involved. Conversely, a lack of relational skills is a predictor of relational trouble. Bad manners hurt feelings, hurt feelings hurt relationships, and hurt relationships hurt lives. The insensitivity of a spouse, partner, friend, or colleague is a major cause of conflict and a threat to the serenity, contentment, and happiness of both parties. In fact, a relationship may not survive the salvos of gross incivility.

It Poisons the Workplace

Regardless of the goods and services they produce and offer, our workplaces are very reliable providers of rudeness. Numbering in the billions, acts of workplace incivility are a serious threat to our quality of life. Large percentages of workers say it is important to them to be part of a civil environment, yet they find that when it comes to civility, their workplaces leave much to be desired. Ninety percent of American workers say that they have been victims of incivility at work, and 13 percent left their companies on account of an incident of rudeness. About four out of ten say they · have worked for an abusive supervisor or employer. One study's estimate of the work time today's managers devote to resolving workers' personality conflicts is 18 percent (up from 9 percent in 1986 and 13 percent in 1991). That comes to almost one day per week.

Incivility lowers morale and causes illness. We know for a fact that a high incidence of coronary heart disease correlates to working under an unfair boss or supervisor. Sick leave, absenteeism, tardiness, and reduced efforts at work follow as a matter of course. Sabotage is an extreme but not infrequent effect as well. Productivity is inevitably compromised, and so is the retention of good workers.

DULY NOTED: The Cost of Rudeness

About 1 million U.S. workers miss work every day because of workplace stress. And "people issues" are the number one cause of workplace stress. The total annual cost of stress to the American economy is about $300 billion.

Veteran professional observers concur with the shopper on the street that the quality of retail service has substantially declined during the last three decades. Most Americans say that rude treatment from salespeople is a common occurrence. We used to notice when service was bad; now we notice when it's good. Companies lose millions of dollars in sales as customers who are badly treated take their business elsewhere. A 2006 survey reported that 46 percent of respondents had stopped doing business for this very reason with at least one company in the previous year. To give salespeople their due, bossy, unreasonable, and self-absorbed customers are equally busy doling out misery to them.

It Escalates into Violence

Incivility and violence are partners. On an Airtours flight from London's Gatwick Airport to Montego Bay, Jamaica, a quarrel over loud singing turned into a brawl involving twelve passengers, causing the pilot to land the plane in Norfolk, Virginia. A Massachusetts moviegoer stabbed another who had asked him to turn off his cell phone. A Virginia man put an end to a long-standing dispute about a barking dog by shooting and killing two neighbors. The typical full-blown road-rage incident begins with someone taking offense at being slighted. This is also the pattern on the streets of gang-ridden neighborhoods, where disrespect leads to bloodshed. In schools as well, taunting and verbal bullying spiral out of control into physical violence. Any attempt at quelling the violence must take into consideration the role of rudeness. When we manage to keep the level of incivility down, the level of violence decreases accordingly.

WHAT CAUSES RUDENESS?

VERY SIMPLY, PEOPLE ARE RUDE WHEN THEY ARE: 1. STRESSED 2. UNHAPPY 3. RUSHED. MORE AND MORE, MANY IN THIS COUNTRY ARE EXPERIENCING ALL THREE AT ANY GIVEN TIME. RUDENESS IS A SYMPTOM OF A BAD STATE OF MIND.

—*ReadyinTX*

This insightful Internet post is a good place to start looking at the causes of rudeness. ReadyinTX might not have the whole answer, but his or her concision has elegance, and the three causes he or she identifies—stress, unhappiness, and lack of time—are major ones. The pithy closing sums it all up: "Rudeness is a symptom of a bad state of mind." In general, rudeness *does* originate in a bad state of mind of one kind or another. When we realize that the rudeness others send our way stems from their own problems, it is much easier not to become deeply upset. We just leave the package of rudeness unopened since it doesn't belong to us. But where does the bad state of mind that makes people rude come from in the first place?

Individualism and Lack of Restraint

GENERATION ME HAS GROWN UP BELIEVING IT'S MORE IMPORTANT TO "DO YOUR OWN THING" THAN CONFORM TO THE GROUP. UNFORTUNATELY THAT ALSO MEANS PEOPLE OF THIS GENERATION ARE MORE LIKELY TO BE INCONSIDERATE OF OTHER PEOPLE.

—*Jean Twenge*

Although it certainly generates innovation, progress, and prosperity, individualism can also be a liability. Someone who goes about the daily business of life strictly adhering to an "I'll do it my way for my own good" philosophy is unlikely to be consistently and scrupulously mindful of others. Certainly the whole extreme individualist's mind-set is not geared toward a genuine appreciation of the subtle points of civil interaction.

Social approval is definitely not as powerful a motivator as it used to be. In part, this is because many of us no longer live in cohesive and controlling communities. We may be tempted to celebrate all this as liberating. When we care little about what others think of us, however, we end up thinking very little of them. We definitely feel less bound by the noble obligations of respect and restraint.

I would not be surprised if a survey told us that a large percentage of people today consider restraint something that does not concern them. In reality, quality of life in a society depends upon the willingness of its members to keep their needs and desires under control. It may be as mundane as lowering the volume of our stereo when the sound can disturb our neighbor or as serious as taking no for an answer when our romantic advances are not welcome. Restraint-based civility makes civilized life possible. In days gone by, good manners were seen as good because they helped make restraint second nature. Values have changed. Self-esteem and self-expression are in; restraint is, if not out, an annoying afterthought. When we lack restraint, we inevitably hurt others and eventually pay dearly ourselves. Think, for instance, about the consequences of car crashes caused by drunk drivers.

Inflated Self-Worth

THE DOMINANT STUDENT DOES NOT SEEM TO HEAR WHAT ANOTHER STUDENT OR EVEN THE TEACHER HAS TO SAY IN DISCUSSION, SO INTENT IS HE ON PRESENTING HIS OWN VIEWS. HE SPEAKS AS IF HE HAS NOTHING TO LEARN FROM OTHERS— OR AS IF THE CLASSROOM DISCUSSION WERE NOT AN OCCASION FOR LEARNING AT ALL. INSTEAD, HE TAKES THE CLASS AS GROUND ON WHICH HE CAN EXERCISE HIS POWER TO CONTROL A CONVERSATION. OTHER STUDENTS FALL INTO RESENTFUL SILENCE.

—Paul Woodruff

Recent studies suggest that we are becoming more self-absorbed. In 2006 about two-thirds of American college students scored above average on the Narcissistic Personality Inventory, a test aimed at measuring narcissism. This is a 30 percent increase since 1982, the year the test was administered for the first time. When the healthy pursuit of self-interest and self-realization turns into self-absorption, other people can lose their intrinsic value in our eyes and become mere means to the fulfillment of our needs and desires. Our self is king, the world at its feet, and we are not inclined to be considerate and kind. Furthermore, when life does not grant us the privileges we expect given the high opinion we have of ourselves, frustration and anger are likely to result, with the attending abuse of innocent bystanders. It is no wonder that, as the NPI investigator W. Keith Campbell observed, narcissists have trouble sustaining close relationships.

Low Self-Worth

WHEN YOU TREAT OTHERS BADLY, ACTING OUT OF ANGER AND LAUNCHING PERSONAL ATTACKS TO GET YOUR POINT ACROSS, YOU'RE ESSENTIALLY SAYING, "I DON'T TRUST MYSELF. IF I ACTUALLY LISTEN TO YOU, YOU MIGHT MAKE SENSE, AND THEN MY WHOLE WORLD WILL START TO CRUMBLE AROUND MY EARS, AND THAT'S SCARY."

—*Kaci L. Koltz*

Just as frequent—if not more so—are the instances of rudeness rooted in a defective self-image. We often deal with our insecurities by becoming defensive and even hostile. It is an unfair game of shifting, in which we make others carry some of our burdens. The high school student who is rowdy and disrespectful? Lacking confidence in his academic abilities, he finds in transgression the only way he knows to "distinguish" himself and remain on his teacher's radar screen. When someone in your life is rude because he has too low an opinion of himself, sometimes your tactful boosting of his self-esteem can make him relax and bring out his best qualities.

Materialism

As Tim Kasser documents in his excellent book *The High Price of Materialism,* people who are dedicated materialists are more likely to show antisocial traits, they are less interested in committing in earnest to intimate relationships, and their relationships are shorter and fraught with conflict. Sometimes we engage in the quest for material gains expecting that money will buy us a better relationship with someone we love. Going the material route to reach meaning and connection usually leads nowhere. The futility of the effort may leave us conflicted and less inclined to be kind to others.

Mental Health Problems

A relatively small (but not insignificant) number of rude incidents can be traced to serious mental health problems. Sufferers from depression and generalized anxiety disorder can behave brusquely and aggressively. Medical literature lists disregard for social norms and for others, irritability, aggressiveness, temper tantrums, and uncontrolled anger among the symptoms of antisocial personality disorder and borderline personality disorder. Recurrent violent and destructive outbursts characterize a recently identified—if not universally recognized—intermittent explosive disorder. And then there are the alterations of mood and the personality changes induced by alcohol or drug abuse. It is not infrequent for addicts to be trapped in self-absorption and to act in hostile ways.

Injustice

UNFAIRNESS BREEDS RESENTMENT, RESENTMENT BREEDS ANGER, ANGER BREEDS HOSTILITY, AND HOSTILITY ULTIMATELY LEADS TO DIATRIBES, DEMAGOGUERY, INCIVILITY AND PERSONAL ATTACKS.

—*Lewis, Wikipedia Talk Archives*

If you talk with him about rudeness, it won't be long before my friend Bill Leeb tells you about injustice. He does not go so far as to say that all rudeness comes from the perception of being unfairly treated. However, he is so awed by injustice's power to stir emotions that he isn't much inclined to look for other causes. The redressing of injustice is a prime motivator in the lives of all people and one of the most powerful forces shaping the course of human history. Untreatable family feuds and blood-soaked revolutions are born of people's conviction that they have been wronged. When we perceive that we are not being treated fairly, we become demoralized, depressed, indignant, or outraged. All those emotional states make us act in a number of hostile (although sometimes morally justifiable) ways. Rudeness is but one of the hues in this spectrum of hostility.

When Gavin attempts to understand what is bothering his son, the teenager hurls profanities in defiance. One of the employees Kendra supervises is growing rudely argumentative with her and other co-workers. Seth's brother has not answered his calls ever since they saw each other at the reading of their mother's will. In each of these scenarios, someone has internalized the role of victim of injustice. Without admitting it, Gavin's son resents being disciplined more harshly than his sister is for comparable transgressions. Kendra's employee is convinced that she is the reason he does not get the plum assignments. And Seth's brother has never made his peace with how the family assets were divided.

Here the connection between rudeness and injustice is fairly easy to trace. But when we pursue the possibilities of Bill's insight, we realize that injustice is the ultimate cause in many occurrences of rudeness that seem to have nothing to do with it. I may be rude to you because it strikes me as unfair that you are smarter, richer, or more popular than I am. (Which raises the question: Is perceived unfairness the engine of envy?) Or I may be rude because I am dissatisfied with the human condition as such. In other words, sometimes it is an existential sense of injustice that makes us act out. The paradox is that as we react rudely to perceived unfairness, we are being unfair to people who are not at fault in any way.

When you are faced with persistent hostility, it is always smart to contemplate the possibility that the other person may perceive himself or herself as the victim of injustice. If you find out that the resentment toward you is justified, do make amends.

Stress

BUT BEING TOO BUSY DOES TREMENDOUS HARM. IT PREVENTS US FROM CONTROLLING OUR LIVES. IT INCREASES TOXIC STRESS, MAKING PEOPLE SICK, CAUSING ERRORS AND ACCIDENTS, TURNING OTHERWISE POLITE FOLKS INTO RUDE HARD CHARGERS AND REDUCING THE GENERAL LEVEL OF HAPPINESS IN THE POPULATION.
—*Edward M. Hallowell*

One-third of employed Americans feel chronically overworked, and about half of them have felt overwhelmed in the past month by the amount of things they were expected to do. *Newsweek* magazine reported that 60 to 90 percent of patients seeing a doctor complain of stress-related symptoms. When it came to identifying the causes of rudeness, three out of four Americans attributed a great deal or at least a fair amount of blame for rudeness to people leading busier lives and not taking time for politeness. A pattern in the fabric of our lives that will not disappear or even fade any time soon, stress makes us less tolerant of the flaws and foul-ups of others. When stressed, we can easily become defensive and irritable, which is only one short step away from rude. Whether at work or in our private lives, stress is a major cause or catalyst of hostility, incivility, and bullying.

DULY NOTED: Bus Uncle's Rudeness

The poster person for stress-caused rudeness could be fifty-one-year-old Roger Chan of Hong Kong, who a few years ago became an instant international celebrity as Bus Uncle (*uncle* being the familiar appellative for a mature male in Cantonese). On April 29, 2006, Mr. Chan was riding on Hong Kong's public transportation bus 68X. While speaking on his cell phone, Mr. Chan was tapped on his shoulder, called "uncle," and told to lower his voice by Elvis Ho, age twenty-three. Mr. Chan's six-minute obscenity-laced rant against his timid young challenger was captured on video via cell phone by a third passenger. Then it found its way to YouTube.com, and by early June it had been downloaded nearly 5 million times. The video went beyond cult status in Hong Kong, becoming a popular culture phenomenon. Phrases from the rant, such as "I've got pressure, you've got pressure," became universally recognizable as they circulated in everyday conversation. The incident gave Bus Uncle an iconic status beyond Cantonese borders. For millions of people around the world, he became the flesh-and-blood emblem of the ubiquitous stress in contemporary societies and its unfortunate consequences—verbally abusive and threatening behavior among them.

Anonymity

> A BIG PART OF OUR INCIVILITY CRISIS STEMS FROM THE FACT
> THAT WE DO NOT KNOW EACH OTHER OR EVEN WANT TO TRY;
> AND, NOT KNOWING EACH OTHER, WE SEEM TO THINK THAT
> HOW WE TREAT EACH OTHER DOES NOT MATTER.
>
> —*Stephen Carter*

Millions of us spend our workdays in those hives of anonymity that are today's big cities, office-building citadels, and supertrendy technology parks, only to return at night to the anonymity of our manicured suburban residential developments. Every day we encounter legions of strangers who will remain strangers. Soulless extras in our life stories, they hardly seem to warrant a nod of acknowledgment—let alone a kind word. In fact, we can easily get away with being rude to them. Gone are the days when the fear of being ostracized was an incentive to be civil: the cohesive social texture which allowed that motivation disappeared long ago. Anonymity gives us the feeling that we can act with impunity.

Not Needing Others

We often fail to make time for people because we do not think we need them—or at least we do not need them in the flesh. Of course, most of us know or at least feel that there is no substitute for in-person contact. At the same time, we also feel that we do not need others that much as long as an alluring and comforting screen keeps burning bright at the very heart of our lives. We are content in electronic isolation. This is not exactly a strong incentive to work on our social skills. But what about the never-ending and ever-increasing exchange of messages in cyberspace? Doesn't that show that we need others? True, these are encounters of sorts. However, if I alienate myself from you online, there are millions of other easily reachable potential respondents. And that is one reason for the often unguarded and coarse way in which Internet conversation takes place. We may need others, but we often want them to remain at a safe distance. We want the feeling that we can connect with them without the burden of having them at our door. The Internet is reconfiguring the meaning of words such as *acquaintance* and *friend*.

Anger

It is certainly possible to be angry and in control. On occasion, we have all been able to express our anger in a calmly assertive and even constructive way. However, poise is often beyond our reach. Overwhelmed by outrage, we rage. Inflamed rather than in charge, we say and do things that hurt people and wound relationships beyond recovery. Incivility—as well as violence—is a frequent byproduct of this kind of expression of anger. It is a sign of a mishandled "bad state of mind."

Fear

And then there is fear—for instance, the fear that comes with a health crisis. Although it is the looming serious illness that makes us angry, our anger can be directed toward virtually anyone. It is not surprising that our victims are often spouses, family, and friends. There are two reasons for this. One is that they just happen to be there; they are targets of opportunity. The other is that when we are threatened by illness, we feel nobody can help because nobody, not even the people closest to us, can really share our burden. Part of our anger comes from an irrational resentment: "You say you love me, and yet I am alone in this." And so, with our judgment clouded by a sense of the unfairness of it all, we end up saying hurtful things to the very people who have our well-being most at heart.

These different factors can work together to create a rude situation. Stress can combine with anonymity, for example, or a high self-opinion with a low need for social approval. The mixtures can prove quite problematic for family, friends, and co-workers. Let's consider one such situation and how it can be rectified.

PROFILE IN RUDENESS

Mary, a CEO's administrative assistant, is a major concern for Leah, her new boss. Mary takes everything personally and is quick to become defensive. On any given day she is either passive-aggressive or openly hostile. She is known for her surliness and curt replies. When Leah notices Mary's habit of pointing out co-workers' shortcomings, she wonders whether Mary does that to conceal her own—real or imaginary ones. She might be difficult because she lacks a healthy sense of self-worth. It is also likely that the stress of dealing with a new boss has exacerbated her insecurity.

Leah decides that a meeting with her difficult employee is in order. "Mary," she says, "I believe you are not happy and that is affecting the quality of your work. I would like to make better use of your experience as I learn the ropes. You have been here fifteen years and survived two rounds of downsizing. You know your job inside out. I don't know how satisfied you are with your experience here. I want you to know, however, that I trust your judgment, that I have a high opinion of your competence, and that I hope to have you with the company for a long time. So, tell me, am I mistaken or are you not happy?"

Leah's frank and cordial attitude encourages Mary to admit to a deep-seated sense of insecurity. She also admits that the rumor that the new boss had been brought in to fire the deadwood had fueled her anxiety in the last several weeks. She had convinced herself that she would not survive a third round of downsizing. Leah makes sure Mary knows that she made her insecurity problem her co-workers' problem and that a new level of engagement and style of communication is expected of her. She plans to continue making Mary feel appreciated to boost her self-confidence and ability to relate at her best with her co-workers.

DULY NOTED: RUDENESS BEGETS RUDENESS

CHICO MARX ONCE TOOK UMBRAGE UPON HEARING SOMEONE EXULTANTLY EXCLAIM, "EUREKA!" CHAGRINED, CHICO SHOT BACK, "YOU DOAN SMELLA SO GOOD YOURSELF!"

—*Richard Lederer*

Although Chico's joke belongs to one nimble comedic mind, tit-for-tat responses are universal. It is almost instinctual: rudeness begets rudeness just as politeness begets politeness. When it comes to rudeness, however, responding in kind is a clumsily defensive, unimaginative, and usually regrettable option. For one thing, responding in kind makes it more difficult to modify the other person's hostile attitude. If the rude encounter involves a stranger, you never know where escalating hostilities might lead. It is not the initial slight that wreaks havoc. It takes your rude response for that to happen. A protracted rude exchange can do serious damage to your relationship with a friend or co-worker. Rudeness is a two-person crisis from which both opponents need to recover quickly and fully. Adding rudeness to rudeness gets in the way of that healing process.

2. Preventing Rudeness:
Eight Rules for a Civil Life

I DENIED MYSELF THE PLEASURE OF CONTRADICTING HIM ABRUPTLY AND OF SHOWING IMMEDIATELY SOME ABSURDITY IN HIS PROPOSITION; AND IN ANSWERING I BEGAN BY OBSERVING THAT IN CERTAIN CASES OR CIRCUMSTANCES HIS OPINION WOULD BE RIGHT, BUT THAT IN THE PRESENT CASE THERE "APPEARED" OR "SEEMED TO ME" SOME DIFFERENCE, ETC. THE CONVERSATION I ENGAGED IN WENT ON MORE PLEASANTLY; THE MODEST WAY IN WHICH I PROPOSED MY OPINIONS PROCURED THEM A READIER RECEPTION AND LESS CONTRADICTION; I HAD LESS MORTIFICATION WHEN I WAS FOUND TO BE IN THE WRONG, AND I MORE EASILY PREVAILED WITH OTHERS TO GIVE UP THEIR MISTAKES AND JOIN WITH ME WHEN I HAPPENED TO BE IN THE RIGHT.

—*Benjamin Franklin*

IT IS EASIER TO AVOID DISAGREEMENTS THAN TO REMOVE DISCONTENTS.

—*George Washington*

Rudeness is a form of criticism. Smart people don't complain about criticism—they learn from it. So, before doing anything else, ask yourself whether there is something in your behavior that causes people to be hostile to you. Do you usually give little in relationships while expecting a lot? Do you dismiss the accomplishments of others while boasting of your own? Are you sarcastic or overcritical? Do you believe that using people is okay but apologizing is not for you? Is there an edge of arrogance to your everyday demeanor? Find the courage to ask someone you trust: "How do you think most people perceive me?" and "If you could change two things about me, what would they be?" Get to know yourself through introspection and the insights of others. By working on your weaknesses, you will cause positive change in the ways others behave toward you.

The wisest way to deal with ill-treatment from others is by being considerate and kind. I am not arguing that if we are civil other people will *always* be civil in return. I am simply saying that more often than not they will be *inclined* to be. To help you with your self-examination and the strengthening of your relational skills, this chapter presents eight rules for living a civil life. Make them part of who you are. There is a good chance that they will do marvels for you and prevent much rudeness.

EIGHT RULES FOR A CIVIL LIFE

1. Slow down and be present in your life.
2. Listen to the voice of empathy.
3. Keep a positive attitude.
4. Respect others and grant them plenty of validation.
5. Disagree graciously and refrain from arguing.
6. Get to know the people around you.
7. Pay attention to the small things.
8. Ask, don't tell.

RULE 1: SLOW DOWN AND BE PRESENT IN YOUR LIFE

WHEN FULLY PRESENT, WE ARE MORE ATTUNED TO THOSE AROUND US AND TO THE NEEDS OF THE SITUATION, AND WE FLUIDLY ADAPT TO WHAT IS NEEDED—IN OTHER WORDS, WE ARE IN FLOW. WE CAN BE THOUGHTFUL, FUNNY, OR SELF-REFLECTIVE, DRAWING ON WHATEVER CAPACITY OR SKILL WE NEED AT THE MOMENT.

—*Daniel Goleman*

We fast-forward, speed-dial, FedEx, speed-date, and dashboard-dine. We race deadlines, channel-surf, and instant-message with a vengeance. Multitasking is a way of life. We run all day, and at night we relax with a fast-paced novel. We live in the throes of speed. Whatever we want, we want it now. The ubiquitous remote control is a reminder of our shrinking attention span and our relentless pursuit of instant gratification. But, as the inimitable Carrie Fisher complained, "Instant gratification takes too long." We are often so consumed with our personal race that we do not feel we have the time to notice the world around us and relate to it in meaningful ways. As Edward Hallowell, an expert on attention deficit/hyperactivity disorder, has observed, kindness requires time and we don't have it. Hurried, harried, and coarse becomes the new standard. Do you feel the need to find a better balance between taking care of business and caring for people, including yourself? As you slow down, your levels of stress go down, which will enable you to value others more and to behave more considerately toward them. Prepare to enjoy their responding in kind.

In the French fable "The Magic Thread," Peter is a restless boy unable to enjoy whatever he is doing and forever daydreaming of the future. One day an old woman offers him a silver ball from which hangs a silken golden thread. She tells him that that is his life thread and that if he pulls it just a little, an hour will seem to him like a second. The thread, she warns him, can only be pulled out, never pushed back into the ball. Peter accepts the magic gift and, from that moment on, goes through life pulling the thread whenever he feels like it, never having to suffer boredom or work his way through trouble unless he wants to. At the end of his life, however, he realizes that he has had no time to take in what has happened to him, good or bad. When the old woman reappears to grant him one final wish, he chooses to live his life again, this time without the magic thread.

Although we have no magic threads, we all share Peter's inclination to fast-forward through life to avoid effort and hurt. When we do so, however, we usually find that it was not a good idea. Most of us live our lives like the child in the backseat of the car who keeps asking "Are we there yet?" This attempt at fast-forwarding doesn't work. The child is trying to erase the time separating her from her destination, all the while feeling that it is impossible. Her mistake is believing that the pace of the trip is too slow. In fact, she is the one going too fast. Only by slowing down to the present moment can she find meaning and gratification.

The presence of our future in our present is an essential feature of the human condition. We act with purpose, which provides us with a window on tomorrow. Even so, we must learn to position ourselves effortlessly within each moment, rather than stumbling through time. We can either escape from the moment or stay with it as it unfolds and do something good with it. It is by doing justice to time that we begin doing justice to people.

Crystal is a pediatric nurse who gives wonderfully therapeutic massages to weary veterans of the workplace wars like myself. As she neatly unties two weeks' worth of toxic knots in my muscles, I can't help noticing how she seems totally at one with her work. She is all presence and purpose. For sixty minutes I gratefully enjoy the regenerative power of her gifted hands. So when she ends our session by patting my back and saying softly, "Thank you, P.M.," I am a little surprised. Why is she thanking *me*? *I* am the one at the receiving end of her skillful care. And then, I get it. Having seen how she loses herself in her work, I realize that she must be genuinely grateful not only for my business (in that case she could just thank me when I pay her) but for the opportunity to do what she does so well. Her work is physically demanding, but her discipline and focus make it seem effortless. She is thanking me for an hour's worth of fulfillment in a state of flow. She is construing as a gift my allowing her to help me—hence, her very sincere, very meaningful "Thank you."

Crystal is always smiling, even-tempered, and positive. She is a study in gentleness. Very aptly, her e-mail address contains the word *sunshine*. I am convinced that her ability to find purpose and peace in her work helps her to be well disposed toward others. The emotional rewards that come to her from dealing harmoniously with others reinforce her sane attitude toward her work. I wish that more of us managed to draw vital energy from a virtuous circle such as Crystal's. Her wonderful attitude will not prevent her from ever having to deal with hostility and rudeness. It is, however, helping her build a network of social support that will be a godsend to her in any kind of adversity.

RULE 2: LISTEN TO THE
VOICE OF EMPATHY

WHEN WE MOVE OUT OF OURSELVES AND INTO THE OTHER PER-
SON'S EXPERIENCE, SEEING THE WORLD WITH THAT PERSON, AS
IF WE WERE THAT PERSON, WE ARE PRACTICING EMPATHY.
                    —*Arthur Ciaramicoli and Katherine Ketcham*

THE PERSON AT WHOM WE SMILE, SMILES BACK. IN ONE SENSE,
HE SMILES AT US. IN A DEEPER SENSE, HIS SMILE REPORTS THE
SUDDEN WELL-BEING WE HAVE ENABLED HIM TO EXPERIENCE.
HE SMILES BECAUSE OUR SMILE HAS MADE HIM FEEL SMILE-
DESERVING. WE HAVE, SO TO SPEAK, PICKED HIM OUT OF THE
CROWD. WE HAVE DIFFERENTIATED HIM AND GIVEN HIM INDI-
VIDUAL STATUS.
                                          —*Bonaro Overstreet*

THE MOST IMPORTANT INGREDIENT IN THE FORMULA OF SUC-
CESS IS KNOWING HOW TO GET ALONG WITH PEOPLE.
                                        —*Theodore Roosevelt*

We may be hardwired to experience empathy, but we often neglect to make listening to its voice a serious priority. Sometimes we
grow jaded with age, sometimes our lifestyles are just too busy.
Whatever the reasons, when we do not listen to the voice of empathy or don't act upon it, we diminish our humanity and miss precious opportunities to relate and connect.

I benefited from an empathic connection a couple of years back
while traveling. The gods of standby had smiled on me, but that

meant I was among the last to board the plane. Finding a crowded cabin and no available space in the overhead bins for my carry-on, I walked the whole length of the plane. In the very last row, an aisle seat was available, but there too all of the overhead space had been claimed. As I looked around me wondering what to do, the man sitting in the middle seat said, "I'll put my bag under the seat." He swiftly got up and removed a sizable floppy red bag from the open bin, which left enough room for my case. When I thanked him with genuine gratitude, he smiled and said, "I know the feeling."

That simple, common expression stayed with me long past the duration of the flight. It is when we "know the feeling" the other person is experiencing that we want to help. Nobody made that man inconvenience himself, nor would he derive an immediate advantage from doing so. He probably had his share of problems and preoccupations, yet he was still able to hear the voice of empathy and extend a heartfelt courtesy to someone he had never met before. Being aware of others is where civility begins. To be *fully* aware of them, we must weave empathy into the fabric of our connection. Our best responses to the presence of others in our lives are born of "knowing the feeling."

The empathy of strangers is good for us not just because it makes us feel better about ourselves and about life, but also because it encourages us to be better persons. Empathy is wonderfully contagious.

RULE 3: KEEP A POSITIVE ATTITUDE

THE GREATEST DISCOVERY OF MY GENERATION IS THAT A HUMAN BEING CAN ALTER HIS LIFE BY ALTERING HIS ATTITUDES OF MIND.
—*William James*

Both your present and your future are deeply affected by the mind-set you bring to your daily experience. The way you *think* your way through life ends up *being* your life. Whether positive or negative, attitude is destiny. This evergreen wisdom holds true when it comes to relating and connecting. A positive attitude makes you cheerful, attentive, and helpful, and therefore likable and easy to get along with. Also, the effects of your positive thinking may help you fend off illness, which can strain relationships. As you remain relatively optimistic and resilient through nuisances, defeats, and adversities, you are more likely to spare others the less attractive sides of your personality. Positivity makes relationships better, and better relationships reinforce positivity.

So, if you are inclined to perceive what happens to you through the fog of negativity, make a change of attitude your number one priority. Accept negative outcomes as inevitable parts of life but without seeing them as proof that your *whole* life is a failure. Do not believe that pain or sorrow is forever. "This too shall pass" is a mantra that rarely lies. When I was clinically depressed, everything hurt and nothing mattered. Part of my agony was the possibility—one very real to me—that the hurt might not end. Ever. What if that curtain of misery never lifted? It was a terrifying thought. Then the curtain did lift and the lesson was there for the taking: pain is not forever. If we are smart, we will face the toughest of times with full awareness of this simple truth. Life is hard but not unbearable, wrote the Italian novelist Piero Chiara. This is so in part because pain is a houseguest and we can look forward to the day when he packs up and leaves.

Always find a nugget of opportunity in the rubble of adversity. (It is always there—somewhere.) Disasters are much more common in our minds than they are in reality anyway. Don't let unrealistic fears haunt you. Make an inventory of the good things you have going for you, and nurture your gratitude. Learn to come to terms with your past, believe that you are able to influence your present for the better, and look at your future as brimming with positive possibilities.

This is a lot to ask of yourself, so don't expect that the change will take place overnight. You may have acquired your negative attitude from your parents during your formative years and now need to undergo a process of unlearning that requires patience and tolerance. If negativity and anxiety have such a grip on you that you have trouble enjoying life, seeking the counsel of a mental-health professional may be the smartest thing you can do for yourself.

RULE 4: RESPECT OTHERS AND GRANT THEM PLENTY OF VALIDATION

> BUT I KEPT THINKING ABOUT JENNIFER THE WAY SHE USED TO BE. AS GIFTED AS SHE WAS, IN BODY AND MIND, SHE NEVER GLASSED HERSELF OFF FROM YOU. IF YOU RAN INTO HER, AT A PARTY, SAY, OR DOWNTOWN, SHE WOULDN'T SAY HI AND MOVE ON. SHE'D ALWAYS BE PARTICULAR WITH YOU. SHE'D ALWAYS LEAVE YOU WITH SOMETHING. JENNIFER WOULD ALWAYS LEAVE YOU WITH SOMETHING.
>
> —*Martin Amis*

Especially when young, inexperienced, and untouched by adversity, we tend to see our fellow humans as opportunities to exploit rather than persons valuable in their own right. How much pleasure can X give me? How much can I advance my career by associating with Z? People seem there for our excited taking. And so, we end up hurting them *and* us. To mature is to gain a heartfelt understanding that others have value and are entitled to respect and consideration.

Think of all your contacts with others, however fleeting, as visits. This perspective will make it easier for you to say or do something meaningful. You want to show people that you value spending that moment with them. Don't breeze by or be perfunctory if you don't have to. Convey with body language that you are available to talk. When others tell you about something that happened to them, do not jump in to redirect the conversation by saying that something similar happened to you too and then proceed with your own story. Let them complete their thought. Then you may consider telling your story in turn. You may decide not to after all, to let them shine. Follow up on something interesting they told you when you last met. Mention that someone was just telling you about the award they received. Ask about their travel plans and volunteer information they can use. Should they share a concern, listen attentively, respond thoughtfully, and keep listening. Don't just notice things, mention them. "Your Colin played a great game on Sunday!" will definitely register with a proud dad.

When I received the news that my colleague Christian was gravely ill and consequently had resigned from his teaching post, I e-mailed him a few heartfelt—although I don't know how effective—words of comfort. Ten minutes later he e-mailed me back from Paris, where he was undergoing a painful medical treatment. He graciously thanked me for my moral support, adding, "I hope that you are well, although I know that you too have your own problems." There he was, in pain and fighting for his life, and still able to show concern for the much less severe health condition of his colleague. That was quite moving and unforgettable. To me, Christian's e-mail represents civility at its best. His transcending of his pain and fear offers an insight into a profoundly decent soul. Christian has passed away, but that "something" he left with me remains.

Be aware that if you are uncomfortable with intimacy, you may find validating others difficult because doing so brings you closer to them. Do it anyway, and keep doing it. The dread is usually worse than the actual act. While you build others up, chances are that your fear will fade as you continue to be gratified by the positive reactions you receive from them. This thoughtful mode of relating is an enormous improvement on the vapid communication that is the stuff of too many of our daily encounters.

People crave validation in its innumerable forms: respect, approval, praise, consideration, fairness, appreciation, encouragement, understanding, kindness, et cetera. If there are no compelling reasons for denying it, grant validation as a matter of course—with generosity and sincerity. Our perception of ourselves is inevitably shaped by the way others perceive and treat us. Validating words and actions build a sense of worth. They remind us that we are the trustees of one another's well-being, comfort, and contentment.

RULE 5: DISAGREE GRACIOUSLY AND REFRAIN FROM ARGUING

> IF YOU HAVE LEARNED HOW TO DISAGREE WITHOUT BEING DISAGREEABLE, THEN YOU HAVE DISCOVERED THE SECRET OF GETTING ALONG—WHETHER IT BE BUSINESS, FAMILY RELATIONS, OR LIFE ITSELF.
>
> —*Bernard Meltzer*

> YOU CAN'T WIN AN ARGUMENT. YOU CAN'T BECAUSE IF YOU LOSE IT, YOU LOSE IT; AND IF YOU WIN IT, YOU LOSE IT.
>
> —*Dale Carnegie*

Rudeness is the ugly face that disagreement shows when it's mismanaged. When you disagree, focus on the other person's position to gain a full understanding of it and to make sure that your disagreement is warranted. If you are uncertain that it is, seek clarification. If you are sure, express your objection clearly and succinctly. Whenever possible, make it a matter of personal belief or preference, not one of choice between right or wrong. Use polite formulas such as "Maybe there is a different way of looking at it," "I wish I were as certain as you are," "I am afraid I can't agree," "I agree with your premises, but I arrive at different conclusions." Interrupting, contradicting bluntly, raising your voice, intimidating, or using sarcasm is never admissible. Nor should you stoop to obfuscating and lying or attributing motives or intentions to the other person without evidence. And, by the way, you can disagree forcefully and tactfully at the same time. A temperate and deliberate objection always comes with an aura of competence and authority.

How many times have you argued for the mere sake of argument, losing sight of the real issue at hand? How many times have you turned a discussion into an opportunity to make the other person look bad? When you managed to do so, you may have won the argument, but did you really succeed? Success is progress measured against the betterment of a situation, not the defeat of a person. Arguing is not a smart investment of time and energy. It is exhausting, often inconclusive, and harmful to any relationship. To paraphrase Dale Carnegie, your triumph will not endear you to the loser.

The ability to disagree only when necessary—and then with poise—greatly reduces your risk of finding yourself mired in argument. You do not have to *argue*—ever. You can choose to *discuss* any issue, that is, in a civil and dispassionate fashion. There is no need to keep stumbling down the path of escalating animosity.

It was in your early years and within your circles of family and friends that you learned to argue. You learned so well that it became second nature. Even if you wanted to, you couldn't just discard your arguing habit like a moth-eaten coat. An effective process of unlearning, however, is not out of reach. Preparation based upon reflection is of the essence. Start with a radical questioning of your urge to prove yourself all the time. Take a good look at your accomplishments.

Maybe you are a beloved teacher or perhaps a loving mother of a child who turned out to be a good person. Or you might be both. Who you are speaks for itself. Silence your inner critic. Avoid comparing yourself to others.

The next time you are engaged in a confrontation, be aware of the dynamics at work. Stop and think hard about the ritual in which you are participating. Ask yourself: "What am I *actually* doing?" "Is my insecurity pushing me to prevail at all costs?" "Which is more important, that I prevail or that the issue be resolved in the best way possible?" "Am I open to the possibility that I might be wrong?" "Am I even listening to the other person?" "Is he or she offering good solutions?" This is a smart way of handling conflict—you don't have to prevail to be a winner.

Of course, the other person may be unwilling to follow you on this enlightened path and may keep on firing his or her salvos, seeking an old-fashioned "I win, you lose" outcome. Then you can still say: "Let's give this some more thought before we talk again." Your hope is that the pause will inject a dose of rationality into what has been until now an emotional exchange. By keeping the amount of arguing in your life to a minimum, you reduce the opportunities for unthinking hostility to arise and for altercations to take place. If you know how to disagree, you are less likely to encounter rudeness.

One very simple but smart idea in marital disagreements is to avoid retreating behind the wall that is the all-purpose sentence "I don't understand." Elisa complains to Bob about something he did. Bob does not see (or does not *want* to see) fault in it and makes an inevitably ineffectual attempt at defending himself. She dismisses his excuses and restates her displeasure, now in an angry tone. Shaking his head, Bob says, "I just don't understand," prompting Elisa to respond, "Obviously that's the problem," which brings the argument to an impasse. Maybe Bob does not understand why he stands accused, or maybe he wonders why Elisa is making a mountain out of a molehill. Either way, Elisa feels he is denying legitimacy to her perspective. To her, "I don't understand" means "This is crazy" or "You have unreasonable expectations." Clearly Bob is giving up rather than investing time and energy in working through the situation. As Bob retreats in sullen silence, a frustrated Elisa feels her anger increase.

"I don't understand" is definitely not a smart verbal move. It often has the effect of transforming a discussion into an argument. Suppose that Bob changes the dismissive *"I don't* understand" to a goodwill-filled *"Help me* understand." Now he acknowledges that Elisa may have a valid point and pledges to do justice to her way of seeing things. Although not a capitulation, Bob's choice of words suggests openness of mind. Few people of average decency could resist the sterling civility of such a plea. Hearing in it the doubly positive message "I need your help" and "I want to make things better," Elisa is now likely to join Bob in his cooperative mood. They feel less like opponents and more like partners. A positive, quick resolution to the crisis is much more likely to occur.

RULE 6: GET TO KNOW THE
PEOPLE AROUND YOU

Maybe familiarity does breed contempt. But it also leads to care, affection, and love. Although it is true that closeness does not confer immunity from rudeness, we tend to behave better with people we know or with whom we have even a very loose connection. Dividing large schools into small academies where students, teachers, and administrators know one another's names reduces alienation and violence. If the fender-bending driver who rearranges your morning commute turns out to be your next-door neighbor, patience and poise will come more easily. If you have made conversation with the stranger sitting behind you on a plane, your pointing out later that her child is kicking your backrest will be received with less animosity. By getting to know those around you, you expand the group of people whom you treat particularly well and who treat you accordingly.

Whenever a stranger is rude to you and you are tempted to strike back, take a moment to reflect. "If I knew this woman, would I treat her rudely? Would I be so dismissive?" Pretend that the offending stranger is an acquaintance instead, and watch your attitude change. Now you are much less likely to be rude and then to become the victim of her rude response.

RULE 7: PAY ATTENTION TO THE SMALL THINGS

Thoughtfulness is often expressed in acts of apparent small import. Paying attention to the little things helps us show respect, establish rapport, and cement relationships. Here are a few examples: saying "good morning," "please," "thank you," and "excuse me"; alerting a stranger that he or she has dropped something; placing by her front door an elderly neighbor's daily paper that landed on her snow-covered lawn; looking a salesperson in the eye when you say thank you and good-bye; refilling the tank of the car you borrowed from your friend before returning it. Sometimes a detail has the power of leaving an indelible trace in our memories, not *despite* being very small but *thanks* to being so, as you can see from this personal recollection.

The letter from the public relations director of the retirement community was similar to many I had received over the years. It included the date and time of the talk I was soon to give there, directions on how to get to the lecture hall, and other sundry bits of information. As I absentmindedly perused it, the sentence at the very bottom of the sheet caught my attention. It read: "We will have a glass of water available at the podium." Of course it is not uncommon for speakers to find a glass of water at the podium—although I have also given many a speech without that basic comfort. For the first time, however, a host had taken the trouble of reassuring me in advance that the water would await me at the appointed place and time. An act that many would consider almost negligible was made significant by virtue of being put in writing. Here was someone trying to do all she could to make her guest feel welcome and at ease. The message she conveyed was "We value you and your presence among us, and we are thinking of all that you might possibly need. Rest assured that, as far as we are concerned, you will have the opportunity to perform at your best." All I had to do, in other words, was relax and enjoy their hospitality. It was thoughtful professionalism at its best.

RULE 8: ASK, DON'T TELL

Whenever possible, exploit the remarkable power of *asking*. Telling can be perceived as bossy, dismissive, and patronizing. Asking is always validating. Someone is being hostile and rude? Ask what his or her reasons are. Your conflict drags on? Ask what he or she suggests to bring about a satisfactory solution. Reduce the number of your sentences beginning with "You should," "I want you to," and "I strongly believe that." Learn to ask instead "What do you think?" "How would you like to contribute?" "Do you have a strong preference?" When you favor asking over telling, the other person is less likely to become defensive and escalate a confrontation. Furthermore, you may come across innovative and smart solutions you wouldn't have thought of yourself.

Some time ago an administrator at the university where I teach made a curt, nearly abusive call to my department's administrative assistant. The issue was a sum of money we were giving one of our graduate students. Rebecca had filed it as a reimbursement, since the student had paid for his own research expenses and then presented receipts to the department. The rude caller contended that it was an award. The question was not totally academic: awards are taxed, and reimbursements are not.

Rebecca's colleague was enraged because he assumed that she had knowingly filed the transaction under the wrong rubric so that our student didn't have to pay taxes. Essentially, he was accusing her of lying on an official document. Rebecca listened to the rant. She refrained from either lashing out or rushing to her own defense. She simply, and masterfully, replied, "I don't know what you expect me to respond to that." What made that reply great? It was dignified and disarming. It did not say, "Let me tell you what I think about that." It meant instead "Think about what you are saying. Do you realize what you are alleging? What would you say if someone accused *you* of being a liar?" The temperate reply prevented the call from turning into an altercation, it kept the lines of communication open, and it gave the other person the opportunity to switch from an emotional to a rational mental state. It strikes me as a remarkable display of relational skills and professionalism.

Following the eight rules for living a civil life presented in this chapter will make you a more likable person. That likability is a primary factor in determining the quality of our lives can hardly be overstated. Our presence must please for our relationships to survive. Being self-absorbed and unkind is social suicide. If you are likable, you are more likely to receive extra attention from teachers and parents, to have a happy and lasting marriage, to enjoy a strong platform of social support, to be more productive at work, and even to receive better customer service and medical care. The fact is, we can't help liking the likable. Their affability is a promise of harmlessness that gives us repose. It is only natural that we feel encouraged to connect and to establish rapport with them.

To be likable you need to open up to others, and to do that you need to be comfortable with being vulnerable. If your experiences of sharing your intimate world with others have been disappointing, it may be difficult for you to dare to be likable. Maybe your role models were conditioned to hold back, and that conditioned you as well. Seek new models and reprogram yourself. This is something you'll have to learn with time and patience, never losing sight of the fact that the prize is quite remarkable.

PORTRAIT IN LIKABILITY

Since we live on two different continents, my friend Luciano and I see each other only a couple of times a year. As Luciano approaches, his smile precedes him. Before any words are exchanged between us, it says that we are still friends, distance and time apart notwithstanding. I imagine that on the face of this earth there might be a person more likable than Luciano, but if there is, I have not met him or her yet. Everything in Luciano's words and demeanor conveys that his world is made better by your presence in it. He is interested in what you do, but what matters to him is the kind of person he believes you to be. He speaks well of you behind your back to countless people, showing pride in calling you his friend. He has that special, endearing air of those who are both smart and earnest.

Luciano lives in a perennial state of pleasant surprise that so many good things to live for exist, all to be shared with his wonderful wife Maria Rita, his family, and his friends, who for obvious reasons are many. He is genial, gregarious, warm, and yet tactful. Nobody has ever seen him traffic in self-importance. Luciano does not boast. A very successful businessman, he would never let his money dictate whom he sees socially. Generous to a fault, he keeps

- Set the mood. Engage the other person in a friendly manner, assuming that he or she will respond in kind. Acting with the spontaneity and ease of someone who expects to be liked makes you likable—and less likely to be treated rudely.
- Draw people out. Shy people in particular need your encouragement. As a general rule, make others talk about themselves and never speak at length about yourself. We all notice those who take an interest in what we have to say and find utterly forgettable the talkative self-impressed.
- Be predictable in the best sense of the word—loyal and dependable.
- Criticize thoughtfully, tactfully, and only when you see your criticism bringing a real benefit to the other person. Do not criticize others solely because they do things differently from how you would do them. You would be making them feel bad for being who they are, which is unfair.
- Do not wait for people to ask for your help. Offer it as soon as you realize that the need is there.
- Appreciate what others do for you. Kindness *is* or *ought to be* its own reward, but you are still remiss if you neglect to show gratitude.
- No matter how strong the temptation, never say anything mean-spirited.

his house always open to friends. A healthy reserve of innocence keeps him lighthearted. And he is loyal. You know that should you need him, he would be there for you before you even asked. But his greatest accomplishment is that he makes you want to be as good a person and friend as he is.

HOW TO APPROACH AND DEAL WITH
DIFFERENT PERSONALITY TYPES

The strategies you found in this chapter are meant to work with all kinds of people. It makes sense, however, to adjust our behavior according to the personality type of the person with whom we are dealing. Adapted from Andrew J. DuBrin, the next couple of pages contain suggestions on how to approach and deal with eleven common personality types. Far from being an exhaustive tract on the topic, this is just a list of generalities to stir your awareness and point you in the right direction. Also keep in mind that in real life you will deal with people who present a combination of types. For instance, some people are more extroverted at work and more introverted socially. A neurotic individual is also likely to be conscientious, as well as inclined to be closed to new experiences. Although you can prevent a lot of rudeness and hostility by adjusting your behavior in the manners described below, stay away from overanalyzing personality idiosyncrasies in the workplace. Whenever possible, you want to supervise the work, not the person.

1. **The Neurotic.** People of a neurotic disposition are insecure, emotional, inclined to worry, anxious, and easily embarrassed. Approach them in a relaxed, reassuring, and even lighthearted way, making sure that you don't add to their distress with your own tension and fears. By being calm and collected, you convey that you are confident that things will turn out for the best. The apprehensive colleagues with whom you are working on an important assignment will become more optimistic about completing it on time and implementing it successfully. As a consequence, their stress levels will go down, allowing the quality of their contribution to teamwork to increase. However, remember that you

cannot rid them of their neuroses. Sometimes their anxiety may remain in place regardless of your best efforts, so approach them with realistic expectations.

2. **The Extroverted.** Outgoing persons are glad when they have the opportunity to talk about themselves and other people. Be an interested listener, affable in your responses and willing to self-disclose in turn. Andrew DuBrin suggests that you make your conversation about people rather than ideas, things, or data. Let your new extroverted friends know that you enjoyed their company and that you will look forward to getting together again.

3. **The Introverted.** Protective of their privacy, quiet, and sometimes shy, the introverted will be pleased if you can do without much idle chatter. They may go for it as an icebreaker, but thereafter do address their interests, because even the introverted can't resist talking about what matters to them. Talk about ideas, things, and data rather than people. That the introverted are slow to become friendly does not mean that they are aloof, arrogant, or have no interest in you. Don't try to pry them open. Give them time, relating to them on their own terms. Accept as normal moments of silence. A strong rapport awaits you as your reward.

4. **People Open to Experience.** Those with this personality type are tolerant, inclusive, alive with interests, and creative. Share with them new and important information and provide insightful comments on it. Stay away from chitchat and gossip, which are rarely their cup of tea.

5. **People Closed to Experience.** Practical concerns take precedence in people closed to experience, and for them dealing with current issues is of paramount importance. To have an optimal experience with them, don't question their perspectives if you don't have to, and don't introduce an

alternative point of view. Respect their routines, which provide them with a sense of security. Deal with facts and stay away from flights of fancy. Grandiose visions or plans are not appealing to someone who is entrenched in prudence and is, in essence, a negative thinker.

6. **The Agreeable.** Good-naturedly willing to compromise and collaborate, the agreeable may not always have the strongest sense of self-worth, but their life is often good because they are liked and other people seek their company. Respond to their kindness with kindness of your own (they will thrive on your words and acts of validation), and enjoy the relaxed relationship made possible by the meeting of persons of goodwill. However, keep in mind that because they are *ostensibly* agreeing, it does not mean they are *actually* agreeing. Especially at work, you may have to assure them that they can disagree and their doing so won't offend you.

7. **The Disagreeable.** Cold, antagonistic, or outright hostile, deep down the disagreeable are often just insecure. Their unpleasantness may not be a personal attack on you but rather an effort to maintain control. Just listen to them, don't take it personally, stick to the facts, and keep emotion well contained. Patience is a virtue, but so is self-respect, which sooner than later you will be wise to show by asserting yourself. The disagreeable need to know that you are not only clearheaded and temperate but also serious about your boundaries. You will not let anybody cross them scot-free.

8. **The Conscientious.** Conscientious people are a blessing, both in your private life and at work. Part of the blessing is that there is no need to remind them of things to do and deadlines to meet. Do not offend them by monitoring their progress closely. On the other hand, be careful not to take them for granted. Let them know how much you appreciate their dependability.

9. **People of Low Conscientiousness.** People with this trait may be good people and good at what they do, even quite pleasant, extroverted, and agreeable, but their unreliability is their undoing—and it becomes your problem, especially when they work for or with you. Part of the problem is that since they can be very persuasive when they promise they will do something, you may be tempted to relax and refrain from closely monitoring them. Don't. Remind them of the specifications in their assignment. Define unambiguously your standards of quality. Check for progress and confirm deadlines. Explain why you need to rely on a timely delivery. If applicable, mention that more high-profile assignments will come their way depending on their coming through on the present one. When they keep letting you down, be very direct, and list the negative consequences of their cavalier attitude on the team's effort. Eventually, spelling out what the repercussions of their unprofessional behavior are going to be for them may bring the hoped-for results.

10. **Risk-Takers.** In social situations, make risk-takers talk about the daring things they have done in their lives, then mention how risk enters your own life. Ask them what they see as the new big thing on the financial horizon, and whether it's time to invest in it. Find out how they cope with the uncertainty that comes with risk-taking. When they are business associates of yours, disclose early and clearly whether you are willing to commit to a risky endeavor. Do not support such an endeavor solely on account of your need to please them. Risk-taking is for many people a way to cope with personal psychological problems such as anxiety, low mood, or depression. In a personal relationship, risk-takers can be fun but also dangerous. You may be seriously hurt if their risk-taking reaches unreasonable levels.

11. **Risk-Averse People.** A salient trait in people with a low propensity for risk is the need to be in constant control of their lives. Job security, good insurance, safe investments, comfortable retirement, real estate, and reliable cars are all topics of conversation dear to them. Nevertheless, even the most unwaveringly prudent person may be game for some vicarious, page-turning risk-taking. Go ahead and recommend to him or her the financial thriller you enjoyed last summer. At work the risk-averse need consistency and repetition and will be threatened by any hint of change. They can be very dependable if assigned tasks with which they are familiar. If you need them to work on something new, make sure they receive proper preparation. In a personal relationship, expect that they will dig in their heels when life brings change and uncertainty.

3. Accepting Real-Life Rudeness

DO NOT SEEK TO HAVE EVENTS HAPPEN AS YOU WANT THEM TO,
BUT INSTEAD WANT THEM TO HAPPEN AS THEY DO HAPPEN, AND
YOUR LIFE WILL GO WELL.

—*Epictetus*

There is a fascinating, very basic human way of dealing with everyday reality that has major negative consequences for the quality of our lives: We tag each experience in our minds as good or bad. The world is something that *happens to us* and to which we are conditioned to react incessantly. Whether it's a field of poppies or an umbrella that won't open, a compliment from a friend or a long post office line, our evaluations of reality essentially boil down to "This I like," "This I dislike." As we grant or deny our approval, unwittingly but surely we shape our future. The moment we tell ourselves, "It's going to be a stinker today," our day becomes just that. A remarkable knack for finding fault seems to be at the core of who we are. We go through life disliking, disapproving, and complaining. The heat is awful, the humidity ghastly, gas prices outrageous, the commute a nightmare, and the parking always a crapshoot. At the office, the new hire is incompetent, the computer slow, the work mind-numbing, the hours long, the deadlines impossible, the budget ridiculous, the meetings pointless, the clients unreasonable, and the boss a jerk. At the end of the day, the weather still fails to please, traffic is even more congested, and so on and so on.

As we say no to the parts of reality not to our liking, we invest precious energy wishing they were other that what they are. As relentless mental editors of our own lives, we fret at the red traffic light, imagine it already green, and are irked when it has the gall to remain red for another few seconds. The end result is that we have just added needless discomfort to an already challenging day. As we live and breathe stress, we think nothing of burdening others with our complaints. We also end up hurting them, since our frustration has made us irritable or angry. Yes, life can be difficult, but it doesn't have to be as hard as we make it by focusing on the yawning gap between how we expect things to be and how they actually are.

REALITY IS WHAT IT IS

JUST LEARNING TO APPRECIATE LIFE WITHOUT CURSING REALITY ALL THE TIME, AND SO DESTROYING YOUR CHANCE FOR HAPPINESS NOW, CAN BE BOTH THE FIRST AND THE LAST STEP IN YOUR PURSUIT OF COMPLETE FULFILLMENT.

—*Wayne Dyer*

When asked how he is, my good friend the gifted psychotherapist Dan Buccino always answers, "Couldn't be better." He couldn't be better because life cannot be different from what it is. Since it *is,* it can't be better or worse. So we might as well accept it, is the hidden message he conveys with a knowing, philosophical smile. Although it may come up short of our expectations, reality is not inherently defective. It is what it is. As unformed wax, it will receive the impressions of our attitudes. If it appears faulty, that's because we look at it through the gray lenses of negativity.

But what if we managed to shed those lenses? What if, instead of indulging in knee-jerk tagging of experiences, we found it in ourselves to accept them, or at least most of them? Imagine yourself free from the "This I like, this I don't" mentality. Imagine perceiving reality—baby pandas as well as tort attorneys, Roman ruins as well as November puddles—with the attitude "This is what is, it is not awaiting my approval, it comes preapproved for the mere reason that it exists." So much precious energy would be saved! No need now to correct the world in your mind, since the world would not be faulty but simply itself. Annoyances would vanish, complaints decrease. Accepting the weather without tagging it makes it so much easier to be in a good mood on a rainy day. Accepting rush-hour traffic as just itself rather than calling it hellish makes going through it much less stressful. Reform how you speak to yourself and others about reality, and little by little you will reform the way you think and feel about it. Abandon your tired vocabulary of dislike and discontent, and enjoy the difference that makes.

THE PRINCIPLE OF EQUALLY ACCEPTABLE OUTCOMES

Acceptance will come more easily if you can believe in the Principle of Equally Acceptable Outcomes. Although we strive to bring about our preferred outcomes in all circumstances of life, nonpreferred outcomes might work out just as well most of the time. Suppose that you have a strong preference for University X but have a good chance of being accepted into College Y. You fuss, fret, and lose sleep as you imagine your happiness at being accepted at X and your disappointment as a Y freshman. You never consider that although being at Y would not bring into your life exactly what X would, in the end the "bad" outcome may turn out to be as good for you as the "good" would have been. X may have a strong department in the field you are now considering for your major, but Y might give you the opportunity to discover a new and more congenial field. You want tomorrow to be a sunny day because you planned a picnic? Do not rule out that tomorrow's unwelcome rain might bring something unexpected that you will enjoy and maybe treasure.

Develop the habit of loose attachment. Whenever you are looking forward to something and the possibility of not getting what you want occurs to you, stay with that possibility and fully explore it in your mind. Look at the unwanted outcome as one with value and promise in itself, not as a total failure. Pursue in your mind its opportunities, and see where they lead you. If nothing else, this will be good exercise for your imagination. You will stumble upon ideas that you may want to put to use regardless of the outcome of the issue at hand. But there *will* be something else. The ability to believe that something good can follow even from something unwanted will help you reduce your anxiety and accept any outcome more serenely. Not all outcomes are equally desirable. They all have, however, the potential to produce desirable results. If you make your attachment to your desired outcomes loose rather than rigid, your life will doubtless become more balanced.

ACCEPTING THE REALITY OF RUDENESS

As rudeness strikes, relate to it as neutrally as you can. Your boss dismisses your hard work? Your friend seems to take your friendship for granted? Your spouse is more considerate of strangers than he is of you? A salesperson makes an insensitive remark about your weight? Don't fight it and don't fix it—not yet, at least. You don't have to like what happened. Come to terms with it without tagging it. In the meanwhile, you will have acquired a better perspective from which to choose your next step more wisely. This point is crucial. When you accept reality, you do not give up choosing between right and wrong, fighting for just causes, being assertive, or following your preferences. Accepting means that your *first* response will be one of acceptance. First you accept, and *then* you open the door to choice and do what you need to. The beauty of acceptance is that in many cases you discover no action is required. Accepting does not mean approving. It simply means acknowledging that what happened cannot unhappen, which allows you to move on with minimum waste of emotional energy. It doesn't make you weak or diminish you as a person in any way. If anything, accepting is a sign of strength and wisdom.

Working on Acceptance

Your choice is quite simple: to go through life finding fault with the world or to find acceptance within yourself. Try this exercise:

List on a sheet of paper the advantages of embracing acceptance. Picture them in your mind. Are there disadvantages? List those as well. If the former outnumber the latter, you may want to engage in a slowly escalating program that will help you maintain an embracing attitude. Commit to a four-week self-training period. During the first week, practice your acceptance of irritants such as traffic at rush hour, lines at the post office or at the bank, and elevators that stop on every floor. On a scale from A to D, how well did you do in each situation? When you find yourself in the same situations during the next few weeks, grade yourself again and compare. Chances are that you will do better as time goes by. During the second week, up the ante a little. You might add to your list your reactions to your noisy neighbor, to the disappointing and costly restaurant meal, and to an unsatisfactory date. During the third week, see how you fare dealing with more perturbing events, such as your child's act of defiant disobedience, your disappointing feedback from your boss, and your mother's guilt-inducing call. During the fourth week, very-hard-to-accept facts of life may include your former spouse's current lies, your weight and looks, and the life-changing decisions you made over the years.

Throughout your period of commitment, keep grading yourself on your reactions to recurring challenges. This monitoring and the gradual increase of your tasks' difficulty will definitely help you change the way you respond. Just like weight management, however, attitude management is largely about maintenance. The risk that the cloud of stressful discontent will come back to engulf you is real. Repeat the scoring routine if necessary. A lot is at stake. Mastering this extraordinary life skill is one of the smartest things you'll ever do for yourself. Surrender to acceptance for good, watch reality be, and acquaint yourself with daily serenity.

DISTANCING YOURSELF FROM WHAT YOU'VE ACCEPTED

> IF YOU SEE YOURSELF AS THE CENTER OF YOUR WORLD, IT'S HARD NOT TO THINK OF YOURSELF AS A TARGET, JUST WAITING FOR THE DART'S STING.
>
> —*Elayne Savage*

Accepting that something is part of reality is one thing, deciding in what ways that something ought to concern you is quite another. You don't have to own what you accept. You don't have to let the rudeness whose reality you wisely accepted upset you. Feel free to distance yourself from it. Consider it a problem of the person who was rude. It helps a lot if you don't take it personally. Unfortunately, nature programs you to do just the opposite. But your waiter's disappearing act is not intended as a personal slight—he is just having a bad day. And the driver who cut you off during your morning commute was not perversely planning a personal affront. That you were the one who had to brake for his life was mere happenstance. Slights happen to us because we happen to be there. The smart way of coping with them is to keep telling ourselves, "It's not about me," until we really believe it.

DULY NOTED: YOUR PERSONAL PROTECTIVE BUBBLE

The following suggestion comes from Elayne Savage, a psychologist who has written with outstanding clarity and competence on some of the topics with which we are concerned: "Another way to protect yourself from emotional overload is to visualize a plastic bubble around yourself where nothing can hurt you. You have the ability to install or remove the bubble at will. Nobody can get to you while the bubble is in place. And nobody knows it is there but you."

Another effective way to spare your ego an unnecessary beating is to distance yourself from rudeness with the help of a little levity. Find humor in the situation and laugh. Ultimately, laughing is another way of not taking things personally. As you become an amused spectator of your own incident, you acquire perspective, defuse tension, and gain control. Taking things personally is probably the default mode with which you have related to reality all of your life. Embrace the wisdom of reprogramming yourself, and commit to working hard at this life-changing project.

But doing so doesn't bring back the infamous tagging ("This I do not like") from which we started? No, not quite. You *have* accepted the act of rudeness. This *has* allowed you to avoid the initial onrush of stress. You *have* maintained your calm and composure. Now you are simply managing the situation according to what you know about the psychology of rudeness. Since people in a good state of mind are not rude, the person who was rude to you must be in a bad one. The act of rudeness is not an indictment of who you are but a symptom belonging to someone else. It is up to you to decide whether you want to help the other person obtain a better state of mind.

ROAD RAGE AND THE
SYNERGY OF ACCEPTANCES

Suppose you are very sensitive to slights on the road and really dislike undisciplined and uncivil drivers. Especially when you are already stressed, you easily become angry at the wheel. Someday—you're afraid—your anger will cloud your judgment and you will find yourself in the middle of a full-blown road-rage incident. But what if, instead of bringing to the scene the volatile burden of previously accumulated stress, you were relaxed? Then you would be much more likely to accept the incident and defuse the danger. This is when the synergy of acceptances comes into play.

No doubt, like most people, you have run your share of almost-red lights, risking life and limb rather than slowing down in your daily race. Then one day you decide to do your best to accept the reality of waiting. You stop fighting it and just let it be. Red lights cease (most of the time) to feel like perversely timed obstacles in the natural flow of your life and become as natural as the flow itself. Little by little, what you considered a liability—waiting—turns into an asset. Rather than time lost, your pause at the light becomes time found—time for yourself. You start to think of every stoplight as your personal oasis of relaxation, rebalancing, and recreation. As someone said, your red light becomes your Zen light. Now mini stress-reduction sessions await you at major intersections on your way to and from work, and you welcome every single one of them.

Your newly found calm makes you a safer driver. It will be easier for you to accept your encounters with the obnoxious and the raging and manage them rationally. Your poise and positive attitude may make the difference between becoming involved in a serious road-rage incident and serenely and safely reaching your destination. You can provide your own examples of synergies of acceptances. When you accept, tranquillity ensues. In turn, tranquillity can help you accept the next thing that comes along. This is a virtuous circle you can use not only when you respond to rudeness but in all life's circumstances.

Acceptance does not mean being a wimp or rolling over at rudeness. On the contrary, the close cousin of acceptance is assertiveness.

RUDENESS AND ASSERTIVENESS

Downplaying what I want is part of who I am. Over the years, however, I have become better at asserting myself, in part by observing with utter fascination my friends who have a real gift for this key relational skill. Through words, body language, and actions, they establish a presence that cannot be ignored. They are able to refrain from saying yes when they mean no, to make their opinions heard and their needs known. They speak up when their feelings are hurt and expect to be treated respectfully regardless of the circumstances. They do not shy away from confrontations but also seek fair, negotiated solutions. They clearly believe that their claim to well-being and happiness is as valid as anyone else's. And yet they are not self-important or arrogant. I am sure some of your friends and acquaintances fit this profile too. Even if assertiveness doesn't come naturally to you, you can reach an excellent level of proficiency in it by learning from them.

Being assertive is not the same as acting as though you have all the answers. It means that you can accept and be frank about your uncertainty. You can make statements such as "I don't know," "I am not sure," and "I need to think about it before I give you my answer" in an assertive way. As long as you are not afraid to convey what you think and how you feel, as long as you are firm about boundaries you do not wish others to cross, and as long as you are comfortable asking for help, you are assertive. "Would you mind giving me a hand?" is a smart assertive request that all too often we do not make, out of either timidity or pride. Assertiveness is *not* throwing caution to the wind and blurting out the first handful of words that come to mind. Make sure that your response to rudeness is one with which you will be happy not just now but an hour from now, tomorrow, or next week.

Rudeness is someone else's problem foisted upon you. Your new boyfriend has never come to terms with his feelings that life has been unfair to him and nobody has ever given him a break (his problem). Resentful, insecure, and frustrated, he takes it out on you (your problem now). This is a crucial moment. You may either play along or cry foul. By condoning his abuse, you allow him to feel that mistreating you is somehow okay. If instead you make it very clear that his behavior is unacceptable, you put him on notice. As far as you are concerned, your relationship will exist only on the basis of mutual respect and consideration. Your firm stance will either send the two of you your separate ways or set the right tone for things to come. Since relapses are possible, you may find it necessary to speak up again. If "again" turns into "again and again," however, you are sending him the message that he can disregard your words because you are in fact taking his abuse. Lack of resolve on your part gives him license not to change.

In your private life or at work, when you are mistreated, do find the courage to ask yourself whether you are unwittingly aiding and abetting your abuser. The temptation to acquiesce can be very strong. Asserting yourself and saying a firm *no* may feel daunting. Experience, however, teaches that it usually is the right choice—the choice that brings long-lasting satisfaction.

When you assert yourself:

- You give other people an incentive not to be rude to you.

- You are true to your feelings, you feel in control of your life, and you feel good about yourself.

- As you assert yourself, your self-respect receives a boost.

- Others do not have to guess where you stand.

- You defend yourself from people's attempts to take advantage of you.

A FALSE SENSE OF NORMALITY

When abuse keeps coming (from your boss, your spouse, even your children), you may accept it as "normal." That's just how your relationship is—sometimes it hurts. Do not let yourself be lulled into a false sense of normality. Something that has become usual is not necessarily acceptable or normal. If you find yourself in a relationship that hurts, ask trusted relatives or friends to give you their opinion on how you are being treated. Through them you may come to see your situation with a clarity that will motivate you to seek change.

PORTRAIT IN ASSERTIVENESS

A fiercely engaged commentator on the political and ethical issues of the day, Lee is bright, opinionated, and contentious. Although he cares deeply about truth and justice, he seems to have little or no use for the norms of polite conversation. To say that he is direct to a fault is to use one of those understatements he disdains. On the eve of an important international soccer game, he e-mailed me: "A friendly wager for the World Cup. Your beloved (and corrupt) Italian team vs. my courageous and aging French squad."

BUILD YOUR ASSERTIVENESS

Keep a journal tracking your assertive efforts. Jot down brief references to the setting and circumstances, to the pressure you felt from other people, and to your response and your feelings about it. At the end of each entry give yourself a grade (A to D) representing how successful you were at handling that situation. For instance:

FRIDAY, AT WORK

The guys insisted that I join them for the Saturday softball game.

I felt a little under the weather, would rather relax at home all day, and told them I am sorry, I am not game.

They protested that the team couldn't win without me. I *must* go.

I felt I was letting them down.

In the end I gave in not to be judged a spoilsport.

Immediately regretted my lack of resolve—a familiar feeling. Grade: D.

Suppose you managed instead to tell your friends "Not this Saturday, but the next I will be there, I promise." This compromise solution would deserve a C+ or a B–. A cleaner "I just have other plans this week, guys. Thank you, but no" would be an A.

When you face another situation requiring assertiveness, describe it in the same way. Try to record five such situations every day over a period of four weeks. Review your five entries at the end of each day. Any chance to get an A+? Save it for when others appear utterly unwilling to take your no for an answer. In this common form of psychological bullying, people apply pressure by questioning your friendship or your loyalty to the organization. When you manage to keep your composure in these circumstances and remain firm in your determination (for instance, just repeating your "no"), you certainly deserve the top grade. This level of assertiveness is not accomplished overnight. As time goes by and you keep doing it, however, asserting yourself will become increasingly easy.

He and I had spoken of the scandal that had shaken Italian soccer, and it involved mostly referees, club managers, and players' agents. But Lee's characterizing the Italian national team as "corrupt" struck me as unfair. More important, I thought that using the word at all was insensitive. I am hardly a flag-waving Italian nationalist. I love Italy, but I have also been critical of my country of origin and my fellow Italians. This time, however, I could not help taking offense. Maybe I was overreacting, but that's how I felt. Since I do not think that people should dole out hurt for no reason, I decided the next time we met I would explain to Lee my perception of what he probably considered friendly banter.

The wager never took place, but our clarifying conversation did. Without animosity, I said I needed to let him know that his breezily contrasting the courageous French with the corrupt Italians had hurt my feelings. He was utterly surprised but almost immediately offered his sincere apologies, which I gladly accepted. And that was the end of it. I will never regret speaking up. I believe I owed it to myself but also to him. The disclosure of my feelings and his making amends dissolved my residual displeasure and resentment. He now has a better sense of how far he can push the envelope with me before I push back. Also, my bringing the issue to his attention meant that I did not take his words lightly. With my frank objection, I was actually showing him respect.

DULY NOTED: Because We Let Them

During the week she lives in a student dormitory at Syracuse University, where she teaches creative writing, an arrangement that is both cost-effective and loud. "But what can you really do?" Ms. Gaitskill said. "You can't tell an eighteen-year-old to keep it down and turn off Britney Spears or whatever it is that they listen to."

This paragraph comes from a profile of the writer Mary Gaitskill that appeared in *The New York Times*. What extraordinary gauges of the malaise of a civilization little mundane observations can be! Of course you can tell an eighteen-year-old to keep it down, Ms. Gaitskill. With all due respect, I would like to submit that not only can you but maybe you should. If you are still a suffering and self-effacing resident in that Syracuse dormitory, allow me to point out that it is your home as much as it is your students', and that those students need a lesson in civility much more urgently than than they need one in writing.

"Dear students of mine, your God-given right to rock and roll ends at my eardrums. I am here to work—for you, incidentally—and need to rest. I would appreciate it if you did whatever it takes to make this corner of the building quiet." End of lesson, lights out. Why are so many people so rude so often? In part, because we let them be. We do not hold them accountable to a reasonable and fair code of restraint, tolerating as a matter of course behavior that only two or three generations ago would have raised indignation.

4. How to Respond to Rudeness

PERHAPS THE CLASSIC EXAMPLE IN THE HISTORY OF WIT IS THE STORY OF A FAMOUS EXCHANGE BETWEEN TWO EIGHTEENTH-CENTURY POLITICAL RIVALS, JOHN MONTAGU, ALSO KNOWN AS THE FOURTH EARL OF SANDWICH, AND THE REFORMIST POLITICIAN JOHN WILKES. DURING A HEATED ARGUMENT, MONTAGU SCOWLED AT WILKES AND SAID DERISIVELY, "UPON MY SOUL, WILKES, I DON'T KNOW WHETHER YOU'LL DIE UPON THE GALLOWS, OR OF SYPHILIS." . . . UNFAZED, WILKES CAME BACK WITH WHAT MANY PEOPLE REGARD AS THE GREATEST RETORT OF ALL TIME:

> *That will depend, my Lord, on whether I embrace*
> *your principles, or your mistress.*

John Wilkes's quicksilver mind is so brilliant, we may forget that his memorable retort is at least as rude as John Montagu's words. This is a classic example of the instinctive reaction that we should resist in our own encounters with rudeness: responding in kind. If you enjoy clever comebacks, frolic with the stars of the genre (Dr. Mardy Grothe has assembled them in her highly entertaining anthology *Viva la Repartee*), but remember that even when witty, rudeness is still rudeness. We are looking for effective and civil responses. If they happen to be witty as well, so much the better.

A few years back, *The Wall Street Journal* published a sobering story on the demise of politeness in the U.S. Among the many reported examples of rampant rudeness, one jumped out at me. While using a public telephone (remember those quaint precellular-age artifacts?), a San Francisco business consultant noticed a man standing behind her, waiting his turn. In an admirable display of consideration, she informed him that since she had several calls to make, she would let him cut in. Several of *his* calls later, when she finally inquired about how much longer *she* would have to wait, he replied tersely: "I didn't think I had to ask your permission to use a public phone."

Rude enough for you? Brazenly countering kindness with rudeness strikes me as rudeness squared. The article did not say how the woman coped with the slight. I can imagine plenty of people remaining speechless in such a situation. A well-balanced reply to "I didn't think I had to ask your permission to use a public phone" might have been "You don't. The fact is, you are using the phone as if it were a private one. I do believe it's my turn now." Clever but not sarcastic, temperate but assertive, this is the response to strive for. Although it may or may not bring you the resolution you want, it will certainly make you feel better about yourself. This kind of reply is definitely *not* beyond your reach once you learn how to prepare for rudeness.

PREPARING FOR RUDENESS

> SPEAKING WITHOUT THINKING IS LIKE SHOOTING WITHOUT AIMING.
>
> —*Proverb*

No matter where you are, no matter what you are doing, rudeness can happen when you least expect it. So, expect it! Expect that the car behind you in the next lane will speed up as soon as you signal that you are switching to that lane. Expect that in the grocery store parking lot one car will hog two spaces. Not being blindsided by adverse circumstances is good outrage prevention, and it is good rage prevention as well. Is the meeting you are about to attend likely to be stressful? Are difficult co-workers going to be present? What will you say and do if someone behaves rudely? Visualize, reflect, and plan. Know yourself, and remain aware of your vulnerabilities. What are the behaviors of others that are likely to push your buttons? Have them in mind so that you can decide how to handle them at your best. Maybe you want to avoid a situation in which you will face such behavior, or maybe you want to prepare for it. What's essential is that you have given yourself an advantage by becoming your own committee of one on the issue.

WHAT TO DO WHEN RUDENESS
STRIKES: THE 3 + 3 SEQUENCE

When responding to rudeness, keep in mind the 3 + 3 sequence detailed below. The first three points listed are meant to keep you calm and clear-headed. Then, with the next three, you take action. Not all your responses to rudeness, however, will require that you follow all six points. Adapt the template to the specific needs of each situation you are trying to manage.

Cool Off and Calm Yourself. Conventional and even hackneyed advice that works shouldn't be summarily dismissed. So, here it is: to cool off, take a few deep breaths and count to ten (or twenty, if necessary).

Don't Take It Personally. Very often (in traffic, for instance) you just happen to be in the line of fire. There is nothing personal

ANOTHER OPTION: IGNORING RUDENESS

You may want to ignore an act of rudeness in one of the following circumstances:

- When addressing the issue would prove more disruptive than the act itself. During productive teamwork you may not want to upset everybody's charmed moment. In a public place, such as a theater, your reaction might cause a commotion.
- When the need for more time and privacy make it advisable to postpone a discussion. If you're a supervisor, for example, it is preferable to call a subordinate to task when others are not around.
- When you are a guest, out of consideration for your hosts and other guests.
- When your duties as host prevent you from doing otherwise.
- When your reaction could endanger your safety or the safety of others.
- When you believe you are about to lose control of your anger.

in the aggressive driving of the motorists around you. Do not lose sight of the simple truth that what makes people rude is a "bad state of mind" (see Chapter 1). Maybe the offending party is suffering from chronic fatigue, has a child in the hospital, or is afraid of losing his job. Or she may be acting rudely because someone was rude to her. As F. Scott Fitzgerald observed: "It's not a slam at you when people are rude—it's a slam at the people they've met before." Sometimes you will actually know their stressful circumstances. The liberating feeling that *this is not about you* may free you from the need to confront.

Decide What to Do. As you consider bringing the issue to the offender's attention, make sure this is a good time and place to do so. A verbal confrontation is charged and can become heated. You always have the choice to let the slight go unremarked and forget about it or to postpone addressing it. Be careful, however, not to develop the habit of avoiding confrontations altogether. Speaking up may still be your best choice. By doing so you take an active role in handling the incident and convey how you expect to be treated—now and in the future as well. Conversely, by ignoring rudeness, you grant permission for more. Your speaking up also gives the other person a chance to apologize, which will bring a sense of satisfying closure to both of you.

State. Bring the troubling facts to the offender's attention. For instance, if you were being accused of being disingenuous, say: "You doubted my sincerity."

Inform. Concisely and clearly let the other person know the effect of what happened on you: "That felt unfair and hurt my feelings." Such an "I statement" allows you to bring the problem to the attention of the person who caused it without overtly blaming him or her. Here is another example: "When you are thirty minutes late I feel that I am not important." One cannot really challenge that. That's just how the person feels. Compare it with a "you statement": "Once more you showed that you don't value my time and my feelings very much." This is an assumption regarding someone else's attitude. Mind reading can easily be challenged ("Of course I value your feelings . . ."). "You statements" are messy, often causing the "you" in question to become defensive and belligerent. A "you statement" is like a door slamming shut on productive communication. An "I statement," by contrast, makes it easier for the two contenders to move on, stepping into the neutral territory of problem solving.

Request. Make clear that you expect the rude behavior to cease: "I would appreciate it if from now on you are more careful before saying hurtful things."

IN SUM: THE SIR SEQUENCE

To summarize, when responding to an act of rudeness, there are three essential things to do: state, inform, and request (SIR). Namely:

- State the facts.
- Inform the other person of the impact he or she had on you.
- Request that the hurtful behavior not be repeated.

Do so politely, firmly, and unapologetically. And do it sooner rather than later. You will be more effective and won't have to dread the prospect of doing it in the future.

WHAT THE OTHER PERSON WILL SAY

In a perfect world, those guilty of rude lapses and indiscretions would respectfully take to heart your assertive remarks, acknowledge their mistakes, and apologize. In our highly imperfect world, however, you can expect that they will immediately shift upon you the burden of blame.

You feel that you must call a colleague to task regarding his lack of discretion during a business lunch:

"Pat, when you started to bad-mouth our board of trustees, I felt very uncomfortable. Do you think it was appropriate to do that with two important clients like Ian and Alinda at the table?"

Your remarks are fully justified, yet your colleague is quick to play the game of blame shifting:

"Well, well, aren't we just superloyal to the big boys since we received our promotion! What's next? Have you set your sights on a corner office upstairs?"

Such obfuscated handling of criticism is typical, so be on the lookout for it and have a good counterresponse ready:

"Maybe. That, however, does not change the facts. Ian called me wanting to know what's going on. I'm the one who has to deal with it now."

When you assertively point out to them their responsibilities, people will often retort that you are not without blame either. Here are some typical defensive statements of the guilty, together with the skillful replies with which you will hold them responsible for their words or actions:

"I didn't mean to offend or hurt you." The simplest and most effective of answers: "Whether you intended it or not, it happened."

"Lighten up. You're making too much of such a small thing." To those who minimize the import of their slight and accuse you of overreacting, you may reply: "You mean that I am not entitled to feel the way I do?" or "Will you please allow me to be the judge of how small the thing is?"

"But how was I to know this bothered you? You never said anything before." Admit that in retrospect you wish you had done so and add: "Well, now you know and I hope you will keep that in mind."

So stand your ground, deflecting deflections. Ultimately, your success in handling rudeness depends on your ability not to let the other person question with impunity the validity of how you feel.

Julian Responds to Rudeness

Julian is competent but famously absentminded. He is the kind of person who places a pile of three-ring binders on the roof of his car as he pats all of his pockets looking for his car key, then drives away with the binders still on the roof. He gets the job done, but his ways of going about it are somewhat quirky. At meetings, he

F*** YOU: THE ULTIMATE DISMISSAL

A verbal act of dominance and dismissal often perceived as the equivalent of the raised middle finger, the expression "F*** you" elicits knee-jerk reactions of outrage that can get even good people in deep trouble. Look at it wisely as the makeshift projectile of an opponent short on ammunitions. In other words, consider it the other person's problem rather than yours. Those resorting to it show a lack of rational and persuasive things to say. So, whether it comes as a preemptive salvo at the beginning of a confrontation or as a face-saving parting shot by someone who feels he is losing an argument, concentrate on remaining calm and clear-headed. Say: "It looks as though this is not the best moment to settle this difference of opinion. Let's try another time." Then walk away. If you perceive that any reply could endanger you, just walk away. Responding in kind may be a temptation, but it is not an option.

asks the question that no one saw coming. He is guileless, self-effacing, and everybody knows he wouldn't hurt a fly.

Most of his co-workers seem to find his difference endearing, but for one of them it has become a big joke. "Hello, Julian, how are things in your galaxy today?" is the kind of greeting Julian has come to expect of Randall. At the watercooler, Randall is now the official chronicler of Julian's eccentricities: "Hey, boys and girls, have you heard about the message Julian left on the boss's machine?" At first, Julian wanted to look at this behavior as good-humored and harmless. As time went by, however, he started to resent an attention that increasingly felt unkind. Eventually he found no good reason to continue to endure the relentless ribbing. Julian decided he owed it to himself to confront the unprofessional colleague, although he knew it would not be easy.

Julian began, "Randall, your constant teasing has become a problem for me. You may find me amusing, but it is no fun to be the butt of your jokes. I want you to stop. Can you see this from my point of view?"

"Wait a minute, you know I don't mean anything by it. Why are you making such a big deal out of this all of a sudden? Don't you think you are overreacting?"

"This is not about what you mean by it, it is about how you make me feel. I am just not comfortable with the teasing and the joking. Among other things, it can hurt my career. Please stop doing it and just treat me like everybody else."

"I didn't know you felt this way. You never said anything."

"True, and maybe I should have. But I am doing it now, so now it's time for a change."

EXTREME RUDENESS: BULLYING

The generic label *bullying* applies to several forms of physical and psychological abuse having at least two major traits in common. One is that bullies select victims unlikely to defend themselves effectively. The other is that bullying is a recurring or protracted ordeal. No longer a term referring only to school yard taunts and assaults, *bullying* is now fully integrated into the vocabulary of workplace harassment. Victims of bullies in the workplace are usually inferior in rank or seniority to their perpetrators. (A large majority of bullies are bosses.) Workplace bullies snub their victims, fail to share important information with them, and set them up for failure. They belittle their efforts, take credit for their work, blame them for the mistakes of others, lie to them, and abuse them verbally or physically. Also, they pass them over for promotion or threaten them with dismissal. A bully's strategy of invalidation can span the whole victim's employment history. Bullied workers often believe that quitting is the only viable way out.

Workplace bullying harms both individuals and organizations. As a powerful stressor, it takes a toll on its victims' mental and physical health. Just working for an unfair or unreasonable boss elevates blood pressure, increasing the risk of heart attack or stroke. People who receive threats of violence are more likely to suffer from depression at some point in their lives. Victims of bullying spend time at work mulling over their plight, take more sick days, diminish their commitment to the organization, and sometimes become utterly disengaged. In recent years they have also started to sue their organizations over their hardship. As good workers unwilling to put up with the abuse find employment elsewhere, their companies are not just hurt by the loss of talent but are also saddled with the costs of replacing it.

How widespread is the problem? Enough to make us pay attention. Estimates suggest that 25 to 30 percent of U.S. workers are bullied in the course of their employment histories, and that 10 percent are undergoing that harrowing experience at any given time. Gary Namie, who directs the Workplace Bullying Institute, estimates that about seven of ten bullied workers quit their jobs. There is no indication that this picture will improve any time soon.

If you're a leader in your organization, you can help build a workplace where bullies don't thrive. Go on record as a staunch supporter of respectful and considerate interaction. Hire staff with people skills. Make sure that workloads are fair and deadlines reasonable, that stress is not rampant, and that employees feel valued and listened to. Make civility a core value in your organization's mission statement. In conduct policies, explain clearly what constitutes bullying and state explicitly that it is a serious violation carrying substantial penalties. Put in place effective protocols for grievance. Gauge periodically the status of relationships among co-workers by surveying your workforce. Offer seminars on the benefits of fostering a culture of civility in the workplace and on the costs of incivility. Create a Civility Day, Week, or Month. Confer civility awards. In exit interviews, try to determine whether bullying was a factor in the employees' decision to leave.

HOW TO DEAL WITH
WORKPLACE BULLYING

If you are being bullied by one or more co-workers, here are six steps you may take to defend yourself and bring about a satisfactory resolution. Keep in mind that no universally applicable strategy exists. What worked for your colleagues may not work for you. Sometimes you must discover your own way.

1. **Acknowledge.** Admit to yourself that you are being bullied and commit to action.
2. **Tell.** Tell one or two colleagues you trust. By asking them to notice how the bully treats you, you secure your first witnesses. Also, they may know of other workers targeted by your bully. Should you decide to make a formal complaint, your case would be much stronger if other bullied workers lodged their own grievances at the same time.
3. **Record.** Keep a detailed record of your encounters with the bully. Save e-mails and any other documents that can corroborate your case.
4. **Confront.** Confronting the bully to give him or her a chance to stop is an optional step and a delicate matter. Some bullies are not aware of how their behavior affects their victims, and they reform when told. Others need to hear the "tough talk" that Gary Namie advocates. You want to impress upon the bully that he or she will not get away with

pushing you around. You are on the case. This is the time to mention your allies in high places. Still, a substantial number of bullies will not be swayed by your confronting them so forcefully and by the prospect of more trouble ahead. They will reject your allegations indignantly and launch an all-out offensive portraying you to management as a troublemaker who is becoming a liability for the organization. One powerful alternative remains, that of confronting the bully, not alone but as a group. Facing a show of solidarity, a bully will find it more difficult to treat you as an aberrant variable, ignore your demands, or dole out arbitrary sanctions.

5. **Initiate an Internal Grievance and Legal Action.** Discussing the situation with your boss can be your last attempt to receive satisfaction informally. After that you can file a formal internal grievance and/or seek legal recourse outside the organization.

6. **Secure a New Position.** For many bullied workers, securing a new position either within their organization or elsewhere eventually is the only viable solution.

CHILDREN AND BULLYING

We all have in mind the daily taunting, roughing up, and ridicule inflicted by children and teenagers upon weaker, insecure fellow students. No school is immune from this cynical exploitation of vulnerability. Perhaps even more common are snubbing and ostracizing, both of individual students and of groups. These behaviors are not as blatant as the first ones listed, but they are certainly taxing for the victims' sense of self-worth; this is bullying too.

The young victims, whose only fault may be failing a test of "cool," experience fear and humiliation. They become despondent and depressed. They diminish their efforts at school, stop seeing their friends, and skip extracurricular activities. Seriously harassed and bullied children number in the millions. Each month about 280,000 students are victims of physical violence in secondary schools, and 800,000 miss school in any given week for fear of being bullied. In a 2007 survey, 90 percent of elementary school students said they had been bullied, and 60 percent admitted having taken part in bullying.

The last several years have seen cyberbullying become a major concern for parents and educators around the world. About 30 to 40 percent of young Americans responding to recent surveys reported having been bullied online. Every moment of every day, in instant messages, e-mails, and postings, millions of children demean their peers, sully their reputations, threaten them with physical harm, and even call for their deaths. This online mean-spiritedness makes its toxic effects very much felt offline. The anguish and the anger do not disappear after its targets have logged off.

Although not typical, tragic endings to stories of bullying are not unknown either. Bullies have killed in the course of an assault, but they are also responsible for the self-inflicted deaths of victims. In any given year, thirty or forty suicides of school-age children are connected to bullying. In very rare cases, bullied children have exacted revenge by killing their abusers.

A serious antibullying effort entails families and schools coming together to design and implement a comprehensive plan. The Norwegian psychologist Dan Olweus, a pioneer in the field of bullying studies, has endorsed the following action list, based on unwavering solidarity for the bullied and unequivocal condemnation of the bullies.

1. **Commitment**. Secure the antibullying commitment of the principal or head of school and install a committee for the coordination and implementation of activities.

2. **Survey**. Conduct a survey of the student body on bullying and disclose its results to all interested parties at a school conference day and a PTA meeting.
3. **Supervision**. Arrange effective adult supervision during recess and meals.
4. **School Rules**. Enact schoolwide antibullying rules drafted in collaboration between teachers and students.
5. **Class Meetings**. Schedule class meetings with the purpose of countering bullying. The goal of such meetings is to assess the quality of current interactions and discuss ways to improve it. Role playing is a recommended method for investigating the nature of bullying and bringing forward the best possible ways to respond to specific situations.
6. **Teacher-Bully Talks**. Schedule talks between the teacher and the bullying students to emphasize condemnation of the behavior. These serious "stop the bullying" talks become particularly effective against the backdrop of other initiatives, such as the antibullying rules.
7. **Teacher-Victim Talks**. Schedule talks between the teacher and the victims of bullying to coordinate protection efforts and provide support.

Whether your school has a strategic antibullying plan or not, a few basic things can be expected of the members of any educational community. Students witnessing the bullying of other students should not ignore it. School bullies are more likely to end their abuse if those witnessing it ask them to. Students intervening in such a situation, however, must remain mindful of their own safety. Help does not always have to be direct—it can also mean alerting a teacher, a counselor, or a security officer. If you are a teacher, counselor, or security officer, you can prevent bullying by being on the lookout for signs that suggest a child is being victimized. They include unwillingness to go to school, missing school gear, unexpected requests for money, unusually low grades, bruises, disheveled appearance, and ripped clothes. Parents should notify the school if they suspect that their children are being bullied or are bullying others.

Both parents and teachers can have invaluable positive effects on children in their care by giving them skills to prevent and cope with bullying. Here are eight suggestions on how to prepare your children to deal with the situation.

1. **Maintaining Open Communication.** Strive to establish with your children the kind of relationship that makes it natural or at least relatively easy for them to tell you if they are being bullied. Make sure they understand that there is no shame involved. "Be smart, tell an adult" is the message to convey.

2. **Training in Relational Intelligence.** Children trained in relational intelligence at home or at school are more confident and successful at making and keeping friends, two abilities that make them less likely to be singled out for bullying. Socially competent children are better at defending themselves verbally. They know how to sound assertive, which is a preferred tone to use with some bullies. They may also be more inclined to disclose to a friend or an adult that they are being bullied.

3. **Staying Emotionally Disengaged.** Since bullies take their pleasure from their victims' distress, train your children not to show much reaction to the taunting, name-calling, et cetera. Without ignoring the bully, experts in the field suggest, the smart child will refuse—as much as possible—to engage emotionally during the incident.

4. **Using Evasion.** Tell your children that clever evasion can work. Sometimes just responding "I'll think about that" or "I guess you feel strongly about that" and walking away brings the bullying episode to a close.

5. **Not Fighting Back.** Do not recommend fighting back physically. Victims are usually less strong than their bullies, and the risk of serious hurt is substantial. Also, the bullies and their friends may accuse the victims of having started the incident.

6. **Avoiding Altercations.** Avoiding altercations makes it less probable that confrontations will turn physical. *Remember: you want to do all you can to keep the confrontation from turning physical.*

7. **Rehearsing Scenarios.** Rehearse with your children two or three typical bullying scenarios until they know what to say and do in each eventuality.

8. **Walking with Friends.** Encourage your children to walk to and from school with friends and in general to avoid the bully.

A FINAL NOTE

Never respond to rudeness with rudeness. Remain focused on the problem action rather than pointing out character flaws.

Forget sarcasm. Resist the temptation of the snappy or arrogant retort. The ephemeral satisfaction you derive from such responses is not worth the long-term damage they can do to your relationships.

Never threaten. When appropriate, instead of presenting the other person with prepackaged demands, enlist his or her help in finding a solution. Most of us prefer to be asked our opinion rather than to be told what to do. Partnering is a conciliatory strategy that allows the other person to save face. If you don't achieve the desired resolution, do not insist but rather enlist a mediator. Breaking the one-on-one pattern of engagement can bring excellent results.

PART
TWO

Situations and Solutions

In the next six chapters you will find dozens of encounters with rudeness, each with a suggested way of coping. My selection reflects in part the results of collaborative work between the Civility Initiative at Johns Hopkins and the Jacob France Institute at the University of Baltimore. In an informal survey on Yahoo.com, we asked "What act of rudeness bothers you most?" We then ranked the results and grouped into categories the behaviors that appeared most frequently. With the help of information from other civility studies, we then identified within each category a number of rude behaviors. In May 2007 we conducted an online survey on the degrees to which those behaviors were considered offensive. Workers at two Baltimore-based companies and the community of a Baltimore university yielded 608 responses. These allowed us to rank the following Terrible Ten—the top ten rude behaviors.

The Terrible Ten

1. Discriminating in an employment situation
2. Driving in an erratic or aggressive way that endangers others
3. Taking credit for someone else's work
4. Treating service providers as inferiors
5. Making jokes or remarks that mock another's race, gender, age, disability, sexual preference, or religion

6. Behaving aggressively toward other children or bullying them
7. Littering (including trash, spit, and pet waste)
8. Misusing handicapped privileges
9. Smoking in nonsmoking places or smoking in front of nonsmokers without first asking
10. Using cell phones or text messaging during conversations or during an appointment or meeting

With an eye to the Terrible Ten study, I selected rude situations in which many people often find themselves and which are difficult to manage. Chapter 5 deals with rude encounters involving spouses, family, and friends. Chapters 6 and 7 focus respectively on neighbors and co-workers. Chapter 8 addresses the travails of travel, and Chapter 9 discusses customers and service providers. Finally, rude digital communication is the subject of Chapter 10. While you may not find here the specific situation you are looking for, you will likely find advice for a similar one. The situations change, but the principles and strategies upon which they are based do not. Your success in putting Part Two to work depends on how well you have absorbed Part One. I don't expect you to use the solution scripts word for word. These scripts are points of departure for creating your own response when the time comes.

As you imagine yourself dealing with the situations I have collected, you may be thinking it would be hard for you to adopt the solutions that accompany them. They *are* confrontations, after all, and some more direct than others. But why should you feel that you are doing something wrong when instead you are the one who was wronged? The more you believe that you *deserve* respect, the easier it will be for you to *demand* it.

5. The Near and Not So Dear: Spouses, Family, and Friends

ONE OF THE GREAT IRONIES OF LIFE IS THAT MOST PEOPLE SAY HURTFUL THINGS TO THEIR LOVED ONES THAT THEY WOULD NEVER SAY TO A STRANGER, OR EVEN TO AN ENEMY.

—*Leonard Felder*

A main reason family members and friends are rude to one another is the feeling that since manners are formal, we don't really need to bother with them when we are in the company of those closest to us. This logic, however, would make sense only if our words and actions did not have the power to bruise and wound others. In fact, a friend's act of rudeness may hurt more than a stranger's. Taking advantage of familiarity to be frank and spontaneous can be relaxing and altogether wonderful. But that does not include doing away with restraint and consideration.

Think of a time when you were at the receiving end of an insensitive remark from your best friend. Did you stand up for yourself? If you did, it was probably with some apprehension. We are all leery of causing ripples in important relationships. The rule of thumb, however, couldn't be simpler: Whenever it feels like the right thing to do, go ahead and assert yourself. Do not hesitate to remind your family and friends that your self-respect makes you demand respect from others, no matter how close they are to you. Especially between spouses, it is important to clear the air to avoid the poisons of pent-up resentment. Closeness and intimacy are wonderful, but no sane relationship can survive without boundaries.

The holidays bring together family and friends who rarely see one another during the rest of the year and are not used to being under the same roof for an extended period of time. Those with a history of unresolved contentious issues use this time to score points. Grown siblings regress to the competing and squabbling of their youth as they vie once more for parental attention. Unflattering old tags are doled out with brio: "You are still a spoiled brat." "You were always insensitive to Mother's problems." "You never gave Gloria a chance."

Many of the rude encounters in this chapter are staple occurrences at family gatherings. Whenever you are about to attend such an event, spend some time considering the challenges you may face. Will you have to endure affluence flaunting, intrusive questioning, and mean-spirited gossip? As the parent of a sweet but without a doubt underachieving child, will you find particularly tiresome your cousin's long-winded boasting about her children's accomplishments? Being prepared softens the impact of challenges big and small and is your priceless compass as you respond to them.

THE SITUATION. *Your Spouse Takes Your Housework for Granted.* Your husband accepts your long work hours as a matter of course. Tidying up around the house, doing laundry, emptying the dishwasher, vacuuming, and taking out the trash do not even register for him as things that someone needs to do. More to the point, he seems oblivious to the fact that you are the one who has taken care of those things week after week since you began living together.

THE SOLUTION. Choosing a moment when the two of you can talk undisturbed, explain to him matter-of-factly the effects of the current imbalance of duties on you. "Terry, I have been doing our housework all these years, and it's becoming a burden. My job is part-time only on paper, and when I get home I'm exhausted. Church work and volunteering at the hospital take up my weekends. You see how busy I am, yet you expect me to do all of the housework on top of everything else. This makes me feel taken for granted and like a second-class partner in our relationship." When he acknowledges that your request for help is only fair, shift gears from principle to planning and say: "I made a list of chores. Shall we look at it and decide who's responsible for what?" Of course, there is the possibility that your husband will ignore you or fail to deliver on his promises. Then you need to decide if you are ready to fight for the change you want.

THE SITUATION. *Your Spouse Criticizes You in Public.* Today it's about you being too lenient toward your favorite child; yesterday it was about spending too much time at work: Your wife has a habit of criticizing you in front of others. She does not seem to realize that this humiliates you—or if she does, she doesn't care. You endure the treatment for quite some time, but when she sarcastically takes you to task for something absolutely trivial you said at her company's annual office party, you decide to speak up.

THE SOLUTION. At the first opportunity you have to be alone with her, say: "Hannah, nobody likes to be criticized. I know I don't. Your jumping all over me in front of other people as you have been doing lately hurts my feelings. It also makes friends, family, and everybody else uncomfortable. From now on, let's stick to constructive criticism and keep it to ourselves. Okay?"

THE SITUATION. *Your Relatives Ask You Intrusive Questions.* At Thanksgiving your extended family's inquiries about your personal life are as much a part of the festivities as those about the weight of the turkey. Aunt Carla wants to know why another year has gone by and you are still not married. She is disappointed that you didn't bring "that nice young man" who came last year. If you *are* married, she wants to know if a baby is likely to appear soon. "Any job interviews lined up?" is Uncle Bob's question. If you *do* have a job, he is certain to ask you how much it pays.

THE SOLUTION. Depending on the circumstances and your mood, you can give serious, straightforward, lighthearted or humorous, or noncommittal answers to questions such as these. Here are some options. On getting married: "Aunt Carla, I must confess that marriage has not been a priority for me so far. I certainly don't rule it out. If things change I will let you know." About having a baby: "You didn't hear? The storks are on strike, so no deliveries are being scheduled." About having job interviews lined up: "Fortunately not, Uncle Bob. You know how they interfere with my pursuit of the contemplative life." About how much money you earn: "Enough to get by, but I could use more. Any ideas?"

$\backsim$

THE SITUATION. *You Receive Unwanted Help.* The moment she finds out you are pregnant, your sister flips open her cell phone to call her midwife for you. Once again, she sees her own experience as universally applicable and her choices as the ones any sensible person would make. You are annoyed by her assumption that you would follow in her footsteps when in fact you are still considering your options.

THE SOLUTION. Stop her assertively: "Not now, thank you. I will keep her in mind, but I'm not quite ready to commit." Should your sister insist, stand firm and convey the same concept again as many times as is necessary. Also, point out the obvious: There is plenty of time to decide.

$\backsim$

THE SITUATION. *Your Grandmother Revisits Your "Weight Problem."* Bridal radiance, married stability, and prompt pregnancy are what your loving grandmother sees in her mind's eye when she sees you—her thirty-one-year-old, still-single granddaughter. Loving she is, tactful not quite: "Now, dear, you have a great smile, you're smart, and you are funny. It doesn't mean that you have to settle for less than the best just because of your weight problem. You were so slim in high school. Oh, well . . ." Although she has occasionally dwelled on your weight before, her comments really bother you now. Isn't there an unwritten grandmother-granddaughter covenant saying that the former must find the latter nothing short of flawless?

THE SOLUTION. Try a response something like this: "Granny, I may be a couple of pounds over my regular weight. But I wish you wouldn't judge me. It makes me feel that I am a disappointment to you. What do you say we drop the issue of my weight once and for all? Let's talk about something else when we're together."

THE SITUATION. *Your Mother-in-Law Criticizes You.* You hear through the family grapevine your mother-in-law's most recent objections to your parenting skills: "I can't believe last night she fed my grandson tofu balls and then let him cry himself to sleep." You are understandably upset, and when you tell your husband, you discover that he was there not only when she said this but when she criticized you several other times as well. You also find out that he has never defended you. "So," you point out, "you let her bad-mouth me and you didn't even tell me what happened." "I didn't want to upset you," he replies, to which you counter, "It wouldn't have upset me nearly as much if you had stood up for me."

THE SOLUTION. While remaining calm and collected, inform your husband: "If you think I'm doing a good job with our son, I hope that you would speak up when your mother—or anybody else for that matter—criticizes me behind my back." Then, at the first opportunity, invite your mother-in-law for tea and inform her, civilly but frankly: "Theresa, it's only natural that you not agree with everything I do with the baby. As parents, George and I are responsible for those decisions, but we will always take into serious consideration your suggestions. I ask only that you come directly to us, so that there are no surprises, gossip, or misunderstandings."

THE SITUATION. *Your Mother-in-Law Gives Backhanded Compliments.* Instead of a warm "How are you, dear?" at breakfast, your visiting mother-in-law says, "That's such a pretty dress—so much nicer than the one you had on yesterday." You think, "It's going to be a long week," as a couple of barbed replies come to mind: "That's ironic, I liked what *you* had on yesterday much more than what you are wearing today," or "When did you become the family fashion expert?" Either would serve her right, you muse. But then incivility would win out.

THE SOLUTION. This is a situation falling squarely under the "Choose Your Battles" heading—meaning you should let this one go. Your preferred response to your mother-in-law's qualified praise of your taste in attire is the simple and civil "Thank you, I like it too."

THE SITUATION. *A Relative Slights You and Your Child.* At your daughter's high school graduation party, your sister-in-law tells a group of neighbors that you always give your daughter anything she wants. This strikes you as insensitive, but you question whether your reaction is warranted. You dread a confrontation, but pretending that nothing happened seems wrong, so you decide to speak up at the first opportunity.

THE SOLUTION. As you prepare for your conversation, consider that your feelings may come as a complete surprise to your sister-in-law and that she may choose to make light of the incident.

You: Joanne, how do you think I felt hearing you tell our friends that you can't believe how spoiled Karen is?

Joanne: What I meant was that not only you but all of us give our children so much these days.

You: I felt that you didn't like her and that you had a poor opinion of me as a mother.

Joanne: It was just a casual remark. Don't make it more than it is. I think you are a wonderful mother.

You: Well, it really didn't sound like a compliment to me. I'm sure it was a casual remark, but casual remarks can hurt too.

THE SITUATION. *A Houseguest Becomes a Problem.* In his first two days as your houseguest, your brother Jeff has been listening to loud music late at night and leaving cigarette butts on the patio. His rumpled clothes overflow from his suitcase, left open on the floor of his room, and he hasn't been cleaning up after himself in the bathroom. His dirty dishes are piling up in the kitchen. While he seems very much at ease in his new surroundings, you believe that it's time to set a few essential house rules.

THE SOLUTION. Say: "Jeff, I hope you are enjoying your stay. I'm afraid that since there is no housekeeping help here, you will have to pick up after yourself. Also, please make sure the music volume is low, especially in the evening. We are glad to have you with us, but in our home everyone is responsible for keeping chaos at bay." If he takes offense ("I guess I should have known that Big Sis's house was too good for messy old Jeff! Brother Jeff was never very welcome here."), say: "I'm sorry you feel that way, but that doesn't change how *I* feel."

~

THE SITUATION. *Your Child Interrupts an Adult Conversation.* As you try to have a conversation with a friend, your bored five-year-old keeps demanding your attention.

THE SOLUTION. Lovingly but firmly take his hands in yours, look him in the eye, and say: "I am talking with Miss Jasmine. Is there something important you need to tell me right now? If it can wait, you will have to entertain yourself for the next ten minutes. The more you interrupt us, the longer you will have to wait for us to finish. Do you understand?" Keep holding his hands until his answer is "Yes." Then make sure you follow through. Also, have him apologize to your friend for the interruption.

~

THE SITUATION. *Your Child Talks Back to You.* "All the kids in my grade smoke. Quit bugging me." This is how your preteen's challenge to your parental authority sounds today—tomorrow she'll think of another, equally disrespectful crack. Finding it disquieting, you wonder how best to address the issue of back talk as a whole.

THE SOLUTION. Stop everything else and sit down with your child. Say: "The other kids doing something that is bad for them is not a good reason for me to allow you to do it yourself. As long as you are part of this household, your well-being is my responsibility. That, I'm afraid, means no smoking at home or anywhere else. Also, the language you just used is not acceptable. It's not that I don't expect disagreement from you, but I won't tolerate the lack of basic respect. It may be okay for other mothers, but my child will not say to me: 'Quit bugging me.'"

Should she up the ante ("This is so stupid!" "You can't make me," or even "I hate you"), probe gently to discover what may have caused her to behave this way. She may be trying on for size the defiance toward figures of authority she's observed in popular classmates. Or she may be claiming some parental attention at a time when you and your husband are quite concerned about another child. Make her think about the possible causes of her behavior, but then reiterate that you expect it not to be repeated. Not only is it disrespectful but it is also unfair, because you are being a good parent who cares about her child's welfare. Review with her acceptable expressions of disagreement.

- I'm uncomfortable when you treat me like a little child.

- I need to make my own decisions.

- I disagree.

- I wish you respected my choices.

- We have a difference of opinions.

- I wish you didn't do that.

By the end of your conversation, make sure you have her commitment to use such expressions in the future.

THE SITUATION. *Your Child Needs to Learn to Respect Persons with Disabilities.* Puzzled by the sight of a child with a disability, your daughter points at him and asks you: "What's wrong with him?" Although you are not the object of the insensitive remark, you are still the one who needs to respond.

THE SOLUTION. Reply: "Nothing is wrong with *him*. It's his muscles that give him trouble, so he needs a wheelchair. I'm sure he has learned to use it very well. And by the way, pointing at people is not polite. It makes them self-conscious and can hurt their feelings."

~

THE SITUATION. *Your Child Hurts Another Child's Feelings.* At your daughter Anita's eighth birthday party, Kerry, age nine, and Brandon, six, are sharing an orange drink. When Brandon leaves to play with his friends, Anita asks Kerry: "Why do you drink from the same cup?" Kerry points out the obvious: "He's my brother." But Anita does not like the answer. She pauses, and then she says: "No, Kerry, he is adopted." At a loss for words, Kerry looks up at you with big questioning eyes.

THE SOLUTION. Ask Anita why she said what she said. Make her focus first on the consequences of her words: "Anita, how do you think Kerry feels after what you just said?" and then upon making amends: "What do you think is the right thing to do now?" If no answer comes, suggest: "How about asking her if you hurt her feelings?" If Anita still insists that Brandon *is* adopted, simply say: "You know that Brandon and Kerry *are* brother and sister. That's all that matters to us."

~

THE SITUATION. *A Child Utters an Insensitive Remark.* After the Saturday soccer game, you take your eleven-year-old and Danny, a teammate, to a family restaurant for lunch. When the waitress leaves with your order, your son's friend whispers a joking remark based on a racial slur about her. Your son, clearly embarrassed, is waiting for your response.

THE SOLUTION. Rather than tell the boy what *you* think, first make *him* think.

You: Danny, I would like you to think about what you just said.

Danny: What do you mean, Mr. Keating?

You: Just that, Danny. Think about what you said about our waitress, Samantha. Was it necessary?

Danny: Well . . . no, not *necessary*.

You: What else? Maybe it was helpful. Or kind. Or smart. These are other good reasons to speak. Was it one of those three?

Danny: I guess it was just something funny . . .

You: Funny is good. But were you funny, or did you make fun of someone else? I know you know the difference.

Danny: I didn't think about it, I just said it.

You: That's it, Danny. That's the point. There are only a handful of good reasons to speak. To say something that demeans others is not one of them, I am sure you agree. Samantha deserves respect just because she is a human being. Making fun of her is not helpful, kind, or smart—let alone necessary. Do you see my point?

Danny: But she didn't hear me. I didn't say it *to* her.

You: True, and if you did, an apology would be in order. However, do you think it's okay to respect people only when they can hear us? An offensive joke can make the people who *do* hear you uncomfortable and offend them even if they are not the butt of it. Give some serious thought to all this, will you?

⟋

THE SITUATION. *You Have Jealous and Controlling Friends.* If you are like me, you have friends who make you feel that you are not giving them the privileged spot in your life they expect and deserve. They point out that you came to town and did not call. If you did call, you did so just before leaving and *after* you saw all of your *other* friends. You suggest that you meet for Sunday brunch, and they take offense: They want to know what you are doing Saturday for dinner. You play tennis two weekends in a row with a new co-worker? They say, half jokingly, "Oh, how quick you are to forget your long-standing friends!" Guilt is the name of the game. But you are *not* guilty, and you don't want anybody to make you feel that you are.

THE SOLUTION. If the person manipulating you is not very close to you, tell him or her that you have other friends and that since you are planning to spend more time with them, you will be around less than you have been in the past. If, instead, you are dealing with someone whose friendship you don't want to lose, say: "I value our friendship, but I do have other friends as well. You seem to resent the time I spend with them, and that makes me ill at ease. Do you mind if we talk about this?" The message you want to send is that you won't continue to passively play the guilt game. Bringing the issue to the fore is the decisive step toward a positive resolution.

⟋

THE SITUATION. *A Friend Is Interested Only in Herself.* Your friend Nicole is always eager to tell you in great detail what is going on in her life. Whenever you timidly start mentioning your own experiences and feelings, she immediately brings the conversation back to her favorite topic: Nicole. You think that she is a good person, but you are getting tired of being an audience of one and wonder if your friendship has a future.

THE SOLUTION. Say: "Nicole, although I hope I am a good listener, I don't want to be just that. Every time we get together I do more than my share of listening to all things Nicole. In the meanwhile, I never have a sense that you are very interested in me. I want our friendship to survive and grow, but it has to become a two-way street. Are you willing to give it a try?" She may be, and even so she may fail. Or she may take offense. Be prepared, then, to lose a "friend."

THE SITUATION. *A Friend Bypasses You When Offering Your Child a Job.* Your teenage daughter, Renee, can hardly contain her excitement. Linda, a family friend who owns a summer house on the Outer Banks, has hired Renee as her summer-long babysitter. This is the first you've heard of the plan. After listening noncommittally to your ecstatic daughter, you call your friend.

THE SOLUTION. Say: "Linda, Renee told me about your kind offer, but I wish you had spoken to me first. I really think she's far too young for the job. We are talking about caring for two small children all summer long, far from home. It's a great job, and I'm glad you have so much confidence in her, but I can't let her go."

THE SITUATION. *A Friend Proves Unreliable.* Taking you up on an offer made long ago, your friend Steve asks for the use of your ski-resort condo for part of the winter. He promises he'll call soon to discuss mutually convenient dates, but several weeks go by with no word from him. Uncertain about his intentions, you e-mail him twice without receiving an answer. When you call after two more weeks of silence, he says he has been waiting for things to get sorted out at work. You feel that his failing to make contact was inconsiderate. Will he also be unreliable as a houseguest? Irritated and concerned, you can't help reconsidering your original offer.

THE SOLUTION. Do you want to impress upon him as strongly as possible that he was remiss? Are you seriously doubting he should be trusted? Then say: "Steve, you never made contact as we agreed, and when I e-mailed, you did not respond. That left me unable to plan my own winter. I am sorry, but the condo is not available now." You will have to accept, however, that this might hurt your relationship. Are you inclined instead to forgive and willing to give your friend another chance? Be assertive but stop short of rescinding your offer. "I really didn't know what to think when you made no contact. My offer stands, but we need to keep the lines of communication open and stick to whatever plan we put together."

⁓

THE SITUATION. *A Friend Won't Take No for an Answer.* From the start, you weren't comfortable with the idea of combining business with friendship, but you agreed to listen to your friend Dave's pitch out of politeness. At least you're giving him a chance to practice. Then you clearly but nicely say no thank you, but he won't quit trying to close the sale.

THE SOLUTION. Maybe your no was not as strong you think it was, or maybe your friend is testing your resolve. Make an argument with a ring of finality: "Dave, we've been around this many times. I understand how important building your portfolio of clients is for you right now, and I wish you all the best. But you must understand our position too. Georgia and I are very happy with our financial adviser. Sayid has managed our money well all these years, and we've gotten to know him as a loyal friend. Why would we want to fire him? We are talking about our savings and our obligations toward someone who has been great at making them work for us. Leaving Sayid would make no sense. Our decision is not going to change any time soon, so please let's consider this settled and move on."

THE SITUATION. *A Friend Hurts Your Feelings.* You're enjoying catching up with your friend Gina, whom you rarely have a chance to see anymore, in a nice restaurant. You're looking forward to a leisurely dinner and catching up on all her news. But having barely finished her veal scallopine, she asks to be excused because she is meeting another friend for dessert and needs to flag down a cab. Taken aback, you don't know whether to pretend that her premature departure is fine with you or to take your friend to task for her rudeness right then and there.

THE SOLUTION. Say: "Gina, had you told me about this other commitment, we could have rescheduled our dinner. I really wish you had done that. This has turned into a very short visit." Gina may apologize for being inconsiderate. Or she may breezily reply that the two of you will meet again soon anyway. Either way, consider revisiting the incident with her in the next couple of days, telling her how it made you feel and what your expectations are for your future social encounters.

THE SITUATION. *Your Children's Playmate Misbehaves.* Near the beginning of a two-day playdate at your home, you observe your son's friend being obnoxious and disruptive. Harry is bossy and pushy, hogs the most desirable toys, and uses language that you don't want your children to hear. He also teases your daughter mercilessly, bringing her to tears.

THE SOLUTION. Give Harry a crash course on the house rules and make it very clear what will happen if he breaks them. If he continues his reckless misconduct, you will ask his parents to pick him up ahead of schedule. Besides being good for your children—in that it protects them and affirms the values you want them to learn—this solution is good for their domineering playmate, who receives a much-needed dose of adult guidance. Should the time come to call his parents, be prepared. Sending Harry packing may upset and surprise them. Having to pick him up on short notice may also be inconvenient. You were providing great babysitting, after all. Expect them to express their displeasure, ask you to change your mind, or both. "Can't you at least keep him through the night?" The answer is no—you would not have called if this was not something that needs to be taken care of now. Just reiterate your decision ("I'm sorry, it's just not working. I do think this is the best solution") until the parent is ready to head to your house.

⁓

THE SITUATION. *An Invited Guest's Health Problem Becomes Your Problem.* When you call your friend Fran to confirm the time of your son Austin's fourth birthday party, she mentions that her child may have a touch of the flu but will certainly be there: "He wouldn't miss it for the world." This is definitely not what you wanted to hear. Not only are you afraid that your son might catch the flu but, as the hostess, you also feel responsible for the other small guests, who will be exposed to the virus as well.

THE SOLUTION. It's time to be very frank: "Fran, we would love to have Foster, but under the circumstances I wonder if it isn't better for you to keep him at home. I am really concerned about the other children catching the flu." Fran may respond that she doesn't have the heart to disappoint Foster. As you reiterate your objection, add: "Listen, I'll freeze two slices of cake. When he feels better, Foster and Austin can have their own little party together."

6. The Neighbors—Noisy, Nosy, and Nice

I have always found it fascinating that the word *rival* came from the Latin word for *neighbor*. Imagine two ancient Roman farmers owning properties next to each other and separated by a little stream (a *rivus,* which is the origin of the English word *river*). By virtue of living on the banks of the same *rivus,* the two farmers are *rivales*—they are neighbors, that is. But being neighbors makes them also rivals. With whom do we quarrel if not with the people in our own backyard? Neighbors have disputes over land and just about everything else. Feuds between neighboring clans span generations. Border-sharing nations war with one another. Whether he or she shares a boundary-defining river with you or not, your neighbor is always a potential rival, an opponent, an enemy. Words such as *rivalry* and *rival* remind us of the contentiousness that comes with all kinds of proximity.

Disregard for the rightful space of others (and for their privacy and tranquillity) is one of the most frequent transgressions and a most upsetting one. We are territorial creatures, claiming sole control of our own space, whether it is our lawn, our cubicle at work, or the tiny piece of beach covered by our beach towel. When others get too close, we bristle at the perceived threat. An atavistic sense that survival depends on defense of space makes us ready to fight for it at very slight provocation. For the purpose of this chapter, I have widened the notion of "neighbors" to include all sorts of people affecting you by virtue of temporary proximity (and sometimes causing you temporary insanity). I mean the people at the table next to yours at Pizza Pizza, in line at the grocery store, or sitting behind you at the cineplex.

THE SITUATION. *A New Neighbor Changes the Rules.* You and the owners of the other town homes on the cul-de-sac have been placing your recyclables in the same collection spots for the last several years. This morning, however, your own bags are not standing on the grassy spot uphill from your front door where you left them last night. Someone moved them all the way across your lawn to the collection point downhill. Your new next-door neighbor—whom you have not even met yet—has left a note in your mailbox. From now on, no bags of other owners will be placed on the grassy spot near her house. That her property does not include that little spot of ground seems irrelevant to her. Your first reaction is to fight back. We are talking about fair use of communal property, with long-established precedent, you tell yourself. Then again, maybe you should just forget about it. Making a fuss in this kind of matter can easily have unpleasant consequences.

THE SOLUTION. When you see your new neighbor, do stop to talk to her. "Hi, I'm the owner of the unit next to yours. Welcome to the Poplars. I hope you'll enjoy living here. I wish you had told me that the customary arrangement for the recycling bags was not to your liking. It's no problem for me to use another spot. May I make a suggestion, however? When issues like this come up, let's talk before taking action. I'm a great believer in keeping the lines of communication open."

⌒

THE SITUATION. *The New Neighbors Are Noisy.* Although you and your spouse have not met your new next-door neighbors, you are quite familiar with their preferences in entertainment. The loud stereo and television sounds coming from their condominium are becoming a serious quality-of-life issue for you. Both of you have been patiently waiting for things to get better, but now you are starting to regret your lack of assertiveness. Also, had you introduced yourselves when your neighbors moved in, you wouldn't now find yourselves in the position of having to tell perfect strangers to start behaving more thoughtfully.

THE SOLUTION. Purchase one of those attractive cards with a blank interior and a fine painting, an urban photograph, or a landscape on its cover. Write on it the following message: "Dear neighbors, we are sure you don't realize how little resistance the sound from your stereo and TV encounters as it travels through our walls. Would you please keep the volume as low as possible, especially at night? We look forward to making your acquaintance and hope that you'll have a glass of wine (or a cup of coffee) with us later this week. Cordial regards." Slip the card under your neighbors' front door. Will the strategy work? I wish I could give it a fifty-fifty chance, but that may be too optimistic. More pleas may be needed before you see substantial results. Have patience, but don't back down unless doing so feels necessary to protect your safety.

THE SITUATION. *A Neighbor's Dog Soils Your Lawn.* As he walks his two small dogs twice a day, your neighbor lets them stray onto your lawn, where they occasionally relieve themselves. Mr. Stanton picks up what he can, but you still feel that his continually allowing his dogs to be on your property is unwarranted.

THE SOLUTION. At the first opportunity, say: "Mr. Stanton, would you please keep your dogs on a shorter leash so that they won't stray onto my lawn? I know you have your plastic bag, but I wish they would relieve themselves elsewhere all the same. There is plenty of room by the curb, there is the wooded area behind the cul-de-sac, and there is the parking lot. Would you mind training them to use those places?" Expect him to deny your charges or minimally concede that "it might have happened once or twice." If so, reply: "Well, it's no use quibbling over numbers, Mr. Stanton. If you'd be so kind as to make sure that it doesn't happen at all, I would really appreciate it."

⁓

THE SITUATION. *A Neighbor Fails to Control His Aggressive Dog.* Heading home on your daily jog, you see your neighbor's cranky dog sitting by the mailbox and looking in your direction. Luckily, your neighbor is there as well, speaking with another neighbor. As you draw nearer, the dog starts barking at you. His owner, however, is too busy chatting to pay attention to the fuss. As you pick up speed, jogging across the street to keep your distance, the dog sprints after you and is soon nipping at your heels. At this point you slow down, turn around, stand your ground, and yell "Stop." Fortunately, the dog freezes. In the meanwhile, no attempt to control him has come from his owner, who is still obliviously engaged in conversation.

THE SOLUTION. You want to stress the seriousness of the incident for the negligent owner and convey your intentions unambiguously.

You: Did you notice your dog chasing me and trying to bite me?

Neighbor: He's just playing. He doesn't mean anything.

You: He bit into my sock. He could have easily broken skin, and I'm surprised you did nothing to prevent it.

Neighbor:	Nothing happened. The dog just got a bit excited.
You:	Dogs this aggressive are supposed to wear muzzles, and you're supposed to keep them on a leash.
Neighbor:	He wouldn't hurt a fly. He doesn't need a muzzle.
You:	Please make sure that your dog doesn't come after me again.

Should the neighbor challenge you, state that you will contact the authorities about the problem if you need to.

⌒

THE SITUATION. *A Disruptive Child Is Ruining Your Restaurant Meal.* The boisterous small child at the next table has the run of the restaurant's dining room. Although her parents seem blissfully unaware of the commotion, if it continues, you and your companion will not enjoy your dinner.

THE SOLUTION. Keeping your distance from the offending party will make an altercation less likely to occur, so resist admonishing the child to behave. Also resist telling her parents that you expect a reasonable amount of tranquillity, and that if they can't control their unruly child they should keep her at home. Your best option is turning to the restaurant's manager, requesting that he or she approach the parents. The expectation that this kind of problem is for the host to resolve is perfectly legitimate. If the manager is unwilling to help or his or her intervention is ineffective, ask for a table in a different room or just leave.

THE SITUATION. *A Cell Phone Caller Is Ruining Your Restaurant Meal.* At a restaurant with a particularly cramped dining room, your neighboring diner with a booming voice has been on his cell phone, off and on, for the last twenty minutes. You and your dining companion have been very patient, but you realize there is a good chance that the disturbance will continue, ruining your evening completely if you don't intervene.

THE SOLUTION. Ask the restaurant manager to speak to your neighbor. The manager may suggest where he can use his cell phone without disturbing those intent on having a quiet meal. If the caller is a person of goodwill, nothing more should be necessary—he will apologize and put the cell phone away. Should he continue making calls without moving, ask for another table or your check.

THE SITUATION. *Relentless Chitchat Is Ruining Your Concert.* You and your date have been looking forward to this concert for weeks. As soon as you get to your seats, however, it looks as though it's not going to be easy for you to sit back and enjoy the music. Behind you, two young women are loudly revisiting moment by moment the party they attended last night, punctuating the highlights with peals of laughter. Any hope that they would quiet down at the end of the warm-up act is soon dashed. Even the featured star lacks the power to curb their chitchat. Being shy, you hate telling people to behave. So far you have dealt with the aggravation only by casting a couple of disapproving glances, which have proven ineffectual.

THE SOLUTION. When you decide to break the impasse by speaking to the unruly duo, say: "Excuse me, we are all here to enjoy the concert, but your conversation makes it very difficult for me to do so. Would you please keep that in mind for the rest of the show? I would really appreciate it." You may receive a profanity in response, so prepare to deal with it calmly, carefully avoiding escalating the incident. If the nuisance continues, look for an usher or a security worker. Your best strategy may be to ask to move to a couple of unoccupied seats in a different section.

THE SITUATION. *People Are Rude at the Gym.* You know the typical workout-room etiquette breaches: People hog machines, pressure others, answer their cell phones, sit on machines just talking, yell across the room, grunt, don't wipe off the equipment after using it, leave litter behind them, et cetera. What do you do in response to such rudeness?

THE SOLUTION. Bring the objectionable behavior to the attention of the shift supervisor or the manager. You may also suggest signs listing the essential rules of gym etiquette. Tell the manager that you expect the rules to be enforced. If the culprit is someone you know, friendly advice is a possibility. For instance: "I wouldn't take out my cell phone in the workout room if I were you. It's not just the ringing or the chatter people object to. They are wary of the phone cameras."

THE SITUATION. *A Supermarket Customer Breaks the Express Lane Limit.* As you wait your turn at the "15 Items or Fewer" express lane, you notice that there are at least twenty-five items in the cart ahead of yours. You are in a hurry and feel hot under the collar about the unfair extra waiting time you face.

THE SOLUTION. Inform (rather than berate) the distracted or mindless shopper: "Ma'am, there is a fifteen-item limit in this lane. Would you please choose another?" If you encounter serious resistance (which you might expect), ask the cashier to call the shift supervisor. Remain calm. Make sure you do not contribute to turning the incident into a scene. Speak mostly with the store's employees rather than the other shopper. Be ready to accept an outcome you don't like.

~

THE SITUATION. *A Supermarket Customer Advances in Line Unfairly.* You are second in line at the checkout behind a woman disassembling a small mountain of groceries on wheels. Looking around impatiently, you see only long lines or closed lanes. A woman behind you, however, pulls her cart over to one of the unattended registers. At the same time, her husband summons the manager. Keys in hand, the manager strolls to the register, opens it, and prepares to process the enterprising couple's groceries. But how fair is that? *You* are next in line.

THE SOLUTION. And that's exactly what you tell the manager as you steer your cart to the newly opened lane. What happens next depends in large part on his professionalism. He should make sure that you were in fact next, then check you out first. If he doesn't, don't make a fuss but do start to compose in your mind a letter to the store's company headquarters. They need to have a fair rule for this common occurrence, and they need to enforce it.

Preventing Neighbors' Hostility When You Renovate Your Home.

Renovations on your house are scheduled to begin soon, and your next-door neighbors will inevitably be inconvenienced. Trying to minimize their discomfort is the right thing to do. It will also make it less likely that relationships will be strained and tempers flare.

Open lines of communication are essential. Send a note to your neighbors alerting them that your renovation will start soon. Mention the beginning and planned ending dates of the project, the daily working hours, and as many specifics as possible about the traffic and noise the construction will generate. Assure your neighbors that you have instructed your contractor that there must be no spilling over of the site onto their properties. Loud music will not be played, and the noisiest work will not take place early in the morning. The workers will tidy up every night. Include in the envelope two car-wash gift certificates with an apology for the inevitable dust. Make sure that the construction crew follows these guidelines. Also, send an occasional e-mail to your neighbors asking how your contractor is doing and giving updates on progress and estimated date of completion.

7. Workplace Woes

Organizations big and small are starting to pay serious attention to workplace rudeness—if for no other reason, because of its costs. Bosses are the usual suspects. Almost 45 percent of the respondents to a 2007 Employment Law Alliance poll said that they had worked for an abusive supervisor or employer. Work today, however, is a near-perfect stress-producing experience for all involved. Job security is a thing of the past and cost cutting the new name of the game. As workloads increase, death-march deadlines that would never have been imposed only ten or fifteen years ago are becoming the norm. Keeping abreast of new technology is a job in and of itself. Energy-sapping commutes are made harder by the ever-expanding rush hour. Many of us are logging a growing number of extra hours scavenged from what used to be downtime. Leisure-starved, sleep-deprived, chronically fatigued, overcommitted, and ultimately overwhelmed, we're hardly inclined to be congenial and considerate, regardless of the rung of the corporate ladder on which we precariously stand.

THE SITUATION. *Your Boss Reprimands You in Public.* The first time your boss rebukes you in front of several workers you supervise, you are deeply embarrassed but decide to just take the bitter medicine. Then he does it again. You know that these scenes will not vanish from your staff's minds, and as you wonder about their possible repercussions on your ability to be an effective leader, you decide you can't afford to ignore the behavior. Tough as he is, your boss has the reputation of being approachable and a fair listener. So now you are in his office, taking a chance.

THE SOLUTION. First, admit that his criticism of your work may have had merit and tell him the corrective steps you have been taking. Then ask if his upbraiding you twice in front of your staff had a significance you should be aware of. If he says that it didn't matter to him who was around at the time, explain that it matters to you. If you can be frank without fear of retaliatory action, say: "I would appreciate it very much if in the future when you have a criticism you'd call me to your office. For my unit to be productive, I need my staff's respect."

THE SITUATION. *Your Colleague in the Next Cubicle Is Noisy.* The co-worker in the cubicle next to yours is oblivious to the fact that his unnecessary noise prevents you from doing your own work.

THE SOLUTION. Say: "Alvaro, you know how these cubicles are. With the constant stream of loud talk coming from your side, it is very difficult for me to concentrate and take care of business. It would help a lot if you held your meetings in the conference room. Also, would you please lower your voice when you're on the phone? I'd really appreciate it."

THE SITUATION. *Your Colleague Takes Over a Shared Office.* Several times a day co-workers stop by to exchange office gossip with your colleague Joan. You think this is inappropriate and resent the distractions and interruptions.

THE SOLUTION. Tell your office mate frankly that you need quiet to work and that you hope she will respect that. She may respond that she had no idea you felt like that and she will put an end to the socializing. Should she instead challenge your request, remain firm in your determination:

> Joan: We're just shooting the breeze. It's no skin off your nose.

> You: You mean that I have no right to feel the way I do?

> Joan: You're making such a big deal about it.

> You: I am simply bringing to your attention something that matters to me.

> Joan: Do you want me to tell people that my office is off-limits to them?

> You: I want you to do what it takes to resolve the situation.

Allow a couple of days for things to change. If they don't, take the issue one rung up the corporate ladder.

⌣

THE SITUATION. *A Supplier Won't Respond.* Your counterpart at a company with which you do business returns your calls belatedly or not at all. Your complaints have brought no tangible results. Since his chronic negligence is not only annoying and inconvenient but also costly, you decide to bring the issue to his attention one more time.

THE SOLUTION. Try an e-mail like this: "Tim, in the past several months I have had to wait too long for you to respond to my calls and e-mails. Although I value your product, the service I am receiving is becoming a problem. At this point I need your assurance that I can really count on you. I do not think that my expectations about promptness are unrealistic, and I want to believe that you will meet them in the future. This will allow our business association to continue. Best, Chris."

THE SITUATION. *A Colleague Makes Personal Phone Calls While Working with You.* Your colleague Trish is a good team player, but she has the habit of using her cell phone for personal calls at work. She thinks nothing of keeping you waiting—sometimes for four or five minutes—while she talks to family and friends.

THE SOLUTION. Find a private moment to talk about the issue. Then say something like "Trish, when you answer calls while we are working together, I feel that I am left hanging and I lose momentum and concentration. Would you mind waiting until it's time for a break before using your cell phone?"

THE SITUATION. *A Colleague Interrupts All the Time.* Whenever someone talks, your colleague Arnold interrupts. Whether it's a one-on-one encounter or a meeting of your unit, rarely does a person manage to complete his or her thought before Arnold takes over. After having observed him in action for quite some time and having been at the receiving end of his behavior, you decide to take him to task.

THE SOLUTION. The next time Arnold interrupts you, make eye contact and in an assertive tone of voice just say: "I am not finished." If he ignores your statement, say again, while maintaining your composure: "I am not finished." If you need stronger ammunition, you can eventually shift to "Arnold, I am not finished. Do you understand? It is not your turn to speak yet. It is mine and I am using it. I will be glad to let you know when I'm done if you have trouble with that." At the end of the meeting, you may want to take him aside and say: "Arnie, nobody likes to be interrupted. People will be more receptive to your ideas if you present them when it's your turn to speak." However, do so only if your familiarity with Arnold allows it. You don't want to be perceived as patronizing.

THE SITUATION. *A Colleague Takes Credit for Your Work.* In an e-mail to every department head, your CEO praises as timely and visionary a state-of-the-art marketing plan for a new and exciting product. Unfortunately, although you and your staff contributed plenty of time, energy, and talent to the plan, you receive no acknowledgment. Why not? Your equal-rank colleague Jeremy presented the plan to the CEO as the exclusive brainchild of his department. You know you owe it to yourself and everyone working for you to fight for the appropriate credit.

THE SOLUTION. Involve your colleague in redressing the situation. Say: "Jeremy, I was dismayed that Corinne's e-mail did not mention my unit's input. She doesn't seem to have been told that the plan is as much our doing as it is yours. I hope you will do the right thing and set the record straight." If Jeremy resists, do e-mail your CEO: "Dear Corinne, I was glad that you enthusiastically endorsed the marketing plan. I am afraid, however, you were not told that my department did all the research on which the strategy depends. It seems only fair that my staff share in the acknowledgment. It would mean a lot if you gave them the public credit they deserve."

THE SITUATION. *A Colleague Keeps Shifting Blame.* Margo is smart and competent but does not seem to realize that working with others requires accepting responsibility as an individual. Anything she happens to do that might reflect poorly on her, she blames on someone else. This constant shifting of blame does not endear her to her fellow department heads. As her mentor and friend, you know it's time to talk.

THE SOLUTION. Say: "Margo, whether you miss a deadline or lose an account, you always point the finger in someone else's direction. But it's *your* deadline, *your* account, and *your* responsibility. Yes, sometimes someone else not doing his or her job will mess you up. But rushing to blame others makes you unpopular, and it does not make you look like a leader. As a department head, you are responsible for your staff's work as well as your own."

⁓

THE SITUATION. *A Colleague Won't Chip In.* Standing at the office watercooler with a paper cup in her hand, your colleague Roger looks around and announces: "It's down to drips." The message is to everybody and nobody in particular. After the announcement, he throws the cup into the wastebasket and leaves without even glancing at the fresh tanks of water stored by the doorway. All he knows is that he is not going to be the one to replace the empty tank. When it comes to that little office chore, Roger holds a perfect record: He's never done it, not even once. You think it's time for him to do his part.

THE SOLUTION. The next time Roger points out that the tank is nearly empty, say immediately: "Let me help you with the new tank." If he responds that he has no time now, just say: "It's only a matter of a minute. Take the empty tank off and then we'll put the new one in together." Of course, he can refuse again, but not without his ruse being exposed.

～

THE SITUATION. *A Colleague Singles You Out for Rude Treatment.* Your colleague Ellen finds every opportunity to show you her antipathy. She is curt and sarcastic, critical of everything you say and do. Although she sometimes uses a tone of superiority with others as well, you seem to be targeted for especially rude treatment. You have no idea what causes this unprofessional behavior, but after enduring it for some time, you want to do something about it.

THE SOLUTION. Begin by working on yourself, trying to keep this from bothering you more than it should. You know that there are times when the stars are just not favorably aligned for good rapport. You cannot be equally liked by everybody and cannot change all that you dislike in others. Imagine yourself floating on the waves of the situation rather than drowning in them. Look at your co-worker as quirky. Demonizing her will just give her more power over you. Distancing yourself a bit prepares you to confront her if that is what you decide to do. Say: "Ellen, I feel that I am not one of your favorite colleagues, and I would like very much to know whether it's because of something I have done or something you have been told about me. Maybe we are not meant to become great friends, but we can still respect each other and work together without dreading every moment of it. Will you help me understand?" Should Ellen decide to open up, the outlook for bettering the situation is good. Should she put up a wall of denial ("I don't know what you're talking about") or just refuse to engage in the conversation, it's time to decide. You may leave things as they are, content with the good feeling that you at least tried. Or you may bring the issue to the attention of someone in a position of authority.

～

THE SITUATION. *You Seem Invisible to Your Supervisor.* For quite some time now your supervisor has failed to elicit your input during collaborative work and dismissed it curtly when you volunteered it. You stop by her office to offer your opinion on a matter discussed at the most recent meeting, but she cuts you off in midsentence. She is too busy to go over this now. You are frustrated and concerned about your future in the company.

THE SOLUTION. The time has come to let your supervisor know how you feel: "Jean, the reason I am here is that at yesterday's meeting I wanted to contribute to the discussion, but I was not allowed to. This is not the first time you did not seem interested in what I had to say. I feel I am in a sort of limbo, and there is nothing I want more than to be treated as a team member. What is your advice?" As you take her to task, remain calm, collected, and civil. Do not raise your voice, dwell on your displeasure, or fan the fire of the dispute with irrelevant accusations. You want to leave the door open for a nonhostile resolution. If nothing constructive comes of this, consider talking to her boss.

THE SITUATION. *You Hear Offensive Jokes.* You overhear a group of co-workers telling jokes that, for whatever reason, you perceive as offensive.

THE SOLUTION. One option is to just leave. Another is to explain why you are leaving ("I find this kind of humor offensive"). A third is to ask your co-workers to stop ("I am not comfortable with these kinds of jokes. Would you please refrain from telling them when I'm around?").

THE SITUATION. *A Colleague Leers at You.* Your co-worker Adam's wandering eyes make you feel ill at ease.

THE SOLUTION. Say: "Adam, I wonder if you realize that the way you look at me is inappropriate. This is our workplace. When we work together, I would appreciate it if you made eye contact with me rather than glancing at other parts of my body. I want to keep our relationship on a purely professional level, and your behavior is anything but that. I hope you understand that this has to change."

⌒

THE SITUATION. *An IT Specialist Is Being Difficult.* You may have lost massive amounts of digital data and certainly won't be able to resume your work until an expert resolves the situation. This problem is serious and upsetting. When you alert Maggie, your technical support person, her answer is "I'm in the middle of something. Enjoy your day off, because I can't help you right now." You feel frustrated and angry about her dismissive and condescending response.

THE SOLUTION. Respond assertively right away. The rest of your dialogue may go more or less like this:

> You: Maggie, I am sure that you have plenty of projects to work on besides mine. However, when you respond as you did, I feel as though you don't care. I need some reassurance that you'll get back to me as soon as possible.
>
> Maggie: Isn't that what I said?
>
> You: No, it isn't.
>
> Maggie: Well, that's what I meant. I'm just busy right now.

You: And I want to impress upon you that this is important to me.

At this point Maggie is more likely to reassure you that she has your problem on her front burner. This is the time to press her for an estimate of when you can expect her to come.

~

THE SITUATION. *An IT Specialist Continues to Be Difficult.* Once again Maggie is very busy. She simply doesn't seem to have time. Ever. She makes people feel they should not ask her to do things that are really part of her job. Claiming to be pressed for time may allow her to appear busier than she really is in the eyes of her supervisor, but she is not fooling you, one of the people she is supposed to support.

THE SOLUTION. Eventually, you must speak up. Say something like: "Maggie, we are all busy here, but you seem to struggle with lack of time more than anybody else. The fact is, if you don't have the time to do your job, we can't do ours. Whether the problem is work overload or time management, maybe you should talk to your supervisor. Like all of us who depend on your support, I really, really appreciate all that you do. However, I want to be able to come to you with my problem without feeling that I am one."

~

THE SITUATION. *A Leader Lacks Relational Skills.* Selina is the head of one of the departments for which you are responsible. Although her knowledge of every aspect of the business is outstanding, she is definitely not clicking with her workforce. She marches into the office every day, head down, reading a memo, and drinking coffee, barely seeming to notice any of her fellow employees. No one dares say hello to her for fear of receiving her cold response or, worse, being ignored. After observing her in action for a while, you decide to speak to her.

THE SOLUTION. Say: "Selina, all of us in the company respect your competence and experience. However, your department would respect you even more if you did a few simple things to build morale. I know they would appreciate your saying hello to everyone in the morning. It's a simple sign of acknowledgment, but it's important. They see you greeting people who come in from other departments and wonder why you are not as cordial with your own. Give the occasional pat on the back. Make your workers feel that they can do a good job, and when they do, show them you noticed. That will make all the difference."

~

THE SITUATION. *A Supervisor Is Being Unfair.* As the head of your department, you are convinced that all your employees should receive a fair number of opportunities to prove their worth as part of special projects. One of your supervisors, however, repeatedly draws from the same pool of talent. Eventually, you decide to bring the issue to his attention.

THE SOLUTION. Your conversation might go like this:

> You: Greg, it seems as though you are not considering certain people when it comes to making up teams for special projects.

> Greg: I consider everybody, and then make my choices.

> You: But those you never choose will never be able to prove themselves.

Greg: Isn't it my duty to field the best possible teams?

You: Absolutely. However, you can't claim you know who really belongs on them until everybody has had a fair chance to shine. Right now you seem to be biased against more than half of your workforce. People do rise to the occasion. Giving new responsibilities to new talent allows you to keep fielding outstanding teams, to retain good people, and to increase morale across the board. I want you to give it a try and let me know how it goes.

~

THE SITUATION. *You Are the Victim of a Snide Remark.* As the overworked departmental administrative assistant hands you the forms you requested, you say: "Thank you, Sandy, I will see you soon," only to hear her mutter under her breath to the secretary beside her: "Not too soon, I hope!" Back in your office, you still feel uncomfortable with her quip and decide to call her.

THE SOLUTION. Say something like "Sandy, correct me if I'm wrong, but you seemed less than thrilled about having visitors in the office today. Did I catch you at a bad time?" Whether Sandy apologizes for her remark or not, she'll probably get the message. You may want to elicit her cooperation: "I don't want to come to your office again feeling that I am imposing. What do you suggest?" She might just ask you to be patient for the next couple of weeks while she completes the departmental budget report.

~

THE SITUATION. *A Relentless Charity Pusher Is Back.* Your co-worker Sharon is making the rounds collecting money for one of her charitable causes. She does this several times a year, and you don't always give. This time, however, you want to, but when you hand over your ten-dollar bill, Sharon informs you that "most people are giving at least twenty." The remark strikes you as inappropriate and insensitive. With your feelings hurt, you are tempted to respond "So go ask them," pocket your money, and leave without another word.

THE SOLUTION. Don't. Just say: "Sharon, this is the amount I'm comfortable contributing. Can you use it?"

⌒

THE SITUATION. *Colleagues Make You Feel Guilty About Your Illness.* After being diagnosed with a serious illness, you tell your colleagues the news. Their considerate responses make you feel good and think that there is healing in disclosure. But then a fellow worker confronts you with intrusive and guilt-inducing questions such as "Did you smoke a lot in the past? Were you a heavy drinker? Have you been overweight for most of your life?" You resent the questions' implication that your condition is the result of self-destructive behavior.

THE SOLUTION. Eventually say: "You know, Angela, those are good questions. However, at this point I am working on getting well, so I prefer to look forward rather than back."

⌒

THE SITUATION. *Colleagues Ask You Intrusive Political Questions.* With the presidential election looming large on the national landscape, you look forward to following the race but not to its repercussions on your workplace. Partisan fervor will make political discussions bitterly unpleasant, workers will make colleagues feel ill at ease on account of their political affiliation, and tempers will occasionally flare. How will you defend yourself from intrusive questions?

THE SOLUTION. Disclosure is not your only option. When asked to present your ideological credentials, you can answer, "Why would you want to know that?" Or "You know, I think that the fewer tags we give one another at work the better." Or "I'm sure I'll make up my mind before election day." Or "I appreciate your interest, but I am really not comfortable discussing such a delicate matter at work." The pressure to disclose can come in passive-aggressive form. Instead of asking flat-out for whom you will vote, a co-worker may play an "outing" game: "And how is our favorite conservative today?" Wrapped in tinny friendliness, it is still coercion, and there is no excuse for it in a civil workplace. If you feel you need to respond, try saying, "And who would that be?" and returning to your work.

~

THE SITUATION. *A Co-worker Attacks You On Account of Your Political Ideas.*

THE SOLUTION. Keep your poise and be assertive. By expressing yourself with determination and self-possession, you will convey the strength of your conviction. You may say: "This *is* my opinion, and I *have* given it a lot of thought," "I would appreciate it if you did not raise your voice," or "Well, let's just accept that we have different opinions about this and move on." The respect you want that person to grant you in future encounters depends on your being assertive today.

8. On the Road, in the Air, and Aboard the Train

Nowhere does today's crisis of ordinary decency make its presence felt more than in the throes of traffic. Here we are, legions of the stressed, strangers to one another, unhappily milling about in lethal steel cocoons. Aggressive driving is everywhere. Risky incivilities such as speeding, tailgating, not signaling, running red lights, and passing on the shoulder are factors in about two-thirds of all crash fatalities. Road rage, the violent response to aggressive driving, is on everybody's mind. And drunk driving, that other potentially lethal incivility, is far from being stamped out.

An exercise in discomfort, anxiety, and boredom, air travel is made unpredictable by multiple factors we can't control, such as weather and traffic volume. Generally speaking, we don't want to travel, we want to arrive. It is not easy to find the fun in long, blank hours spent sharing close quarters with people we don't know who have different views regarding what constitutes acceptable behavior. We have learned to endure philosophically the security ordeal and ill-managed delays. The same is true for overcrowding and spartan service. Being treated like freight, however, remains one of the most humbling and disquieting experiences around.

Train travel, by contrast, remains far more pleasant. Still, plenty of rude behavior and frustrating moments can be found on any of the country's rail routes, from local commuter lines to transcontinental express trains.

Read on for help with rudeness no matter what mode of transportation you find yourself using to get from point A to point B.

THE SITUATION. *Another Driver Is Tailgating You.* For the last two or three minutes, a large SUV has been tailgating you in the left lane. Since you are doing the speed limit, you feel that you are not in the wrong and should be left alone. To stay the course is your right and your intention.

THE SOLUTION. You may be right in the abstract, but that does not necessarily make you safe. The real issue is the smart management of a dangerous situation. Do not brake, and do not start slowing and accelerating to shake off the other car. Turn your signal on and move to the right lane as soon as possible, so that the faster car can overtake you. Do not honk or gesture. Be happy instead that you are off the hook. Now, be proactive. Whenever a lot of cars overtake you on the right, realize that you should probably not be in the left lane. Move to a slower one.

THE SITUATION. *Another Driver Prevents You from Changing Lanes.* About a mile from your exit, you turn your signal on to get into the right lane and eventually the exit lane. As if on cue, the car just behind you in the right lane accelerates, almost closing the gap between you. Prudently, you postpone merging. When the traffic clears ahead of you in your lane, you accelerate and signal again your intention to merge. This only prompts the other driver to accelerate in turn, so that his car is right next to yours. Clearly he sees giving way as a loss of face. As your irritation turns to anger, you are tempted to force the issue.

THE SOLUTION. Don't. No honking, no gesturing, and no swerving. Slow down, letting him pass you, and take comfort in having put safety—yours and his—first.

THE SITUATION. *Another Driver Steals Your Parking Space.* It is Saturday afternoon, and in the grocery store parking lot spots are at a premium. You wait patiently with your turn signal on while a young mother loads her groceries into her minivan and straps her baby into his car seat. As the minivan backs out of its spot, a fire-engine-red sports car neatly slips into it. Images from the parking-lot car ramming in *Fried Green Tomatoes* flash across your mind. You figure that you have two alternatives: Avoiding commotion by quietly giving up the space that should have been rightfully yours is one. Giving the rude driver a piece of your mind and doing what it takes to get your space back is the other.

THE SOLUTION. If you decide to confront the inconsiderate driver, do so in an assertive rather than an aggressive way. It will be a victory just making him or her hear you on the subject: "I had been waiting for that spot with my turn signal on for quite some time. I would appreciate it if you let me have it." If the other driver responds dismissively or aggressively, just say, "I am sorry you are not choosing to do the right thing. I just hope you think about it so the next time you will," and walk away. Do not, under any circumstances, let yourself be drawn into an altercation.

Or you can make your point without confronting the other person. On a piece of paper write: "Dear fellow parker, maybe you did not see me waiting for the parking spot that you currently occupy. If this is the case, please be more aware of your surroundings the next time. If you did see my waiting car and chose to go ahead nevertheless, you owe me an apology. Be kind to someone else today and consider your apology accepted." Fold the paper and place it under the windshield wiper of the parked car.

~

THE SITUATION. *The Infamous Finger Makes an Appearance.* The battered pickup truck in front of you has kept you going at an excruciatingly slow speed in the fast lane. You have been patient, but you finally can't help honking your displeasure. When you do, the other driver's response comes in the form of a raised middle finger. The unimaginative profanity makes you furious. The thinking function seems to be temporarily obliterated from your brain. All that matters to you is not letting your rival get away scot-free.

THE SOLUTION. Bypass your knee-jerk reaction to gesture back, tailgate, or keep leaning on your horn. This is not about getting even, teaching the guy a lesson, or gaining the upper hand. Instead, remain clearheaded under pressure. You don't want to end up reenacting the Ben-Hur–Messala charioteering duel. So here's what to do:

- Whenever you are at the wheel, expect that the infamous finger may appear at some point. Picture the scene in your mind: there you are, calm and collected even after the slight. Anticipating and visualizing make you feel in control and prepare you to deal at your best with the real thing.

- When the offensive gesture does happen, take a deep breath and accept unconditionally that it did.

- Understand that the other person is not gesturing at you— the specific human being you are, with your unique identity—but rather at an anonymous person who just happens to be driving that car at that moment. Making the slight less personal will take some of the sting out of it.

- Do not forget to see in the gesturing a reflection of the other person's bad state of mind. You are in no way required to make his or her problem yours.

There are few things that make us see red as much as a glimpse of that impudently raised middle finger. Condition yourself to deal with it in an intelligent way not only when driving but in all circumstances. This is a matter of self-respect, respect for others, and safety.

⁓

THE SITUATION. *You Are at the Receiving End of Intemperate Honking.* As the traffic light turns green, you linger a couple of seconds, making sure that nobody on the intersecting roadway has gone through the red light. That's when the driver behind you leans on his horn. This startles you. You feel like getting out of the car and telling him why you lingered. That would show him how asinine his impatience was.

THE SOLUTION. Don't. Ignore the intemperate honking, enter the intersection when you believe it is safe, and continue on at your own pace. There is no way to improve upon cool rationality.

⁓

THE SITUATION. *Another Driver Yells at You.* As you exit your parked car, your door hits the door of the car parked next to it. No damage is done, but the other car's owner, who is putting his grocery bags in the trunk, starts yelling at you.

THE SOLUTION. Wait for the outburst to abate, ask to be shown any evidence of damage, say that you are sorry the two doors touched but calmly add that no damage was done and profanity was uncalled for.

THE SITUATION. *Yet Another Driver Yells at You.* When lack of attention makes you rear-end a car stopped at a red light, the car's driver comes at you hurling profanities. You have wrecked his new car, which has only three hundred miles on it. He had important appointments, and now his day is ruined. Someone is going to pay a lot of money for this.

THE SOLUTION. After making sure that nobody in the other car is hurt, bring to the driver's attention that this is a fender bender, that you are insured, and that you want to be on your way as much as he does. Say: "Your car and mine are in working order. There is no reason for us to spend hours here. If we exchange information quickly, you may be able to keep your appointments after all."

THE SITUATION. *A Nondisabled Driver Has Taken Your Disabled-Designated Parking Spot.* As a disabled person, over the years you have found your share of disabled parking spots occupied by cars without the special permit. Today it's happened again. The white sedan parked beside the main mall entrance bears no sign that would qualify it to sit where it does. So you turn around and find a regular spot at quite some distance. Walking back toward the mall, you notice a young woman putting shopping bags into the white sedan's trunk and welcome the opportunity to make your voice heard.

THE SOLUTION. The conversation might go like this:

You: Excuse me, I looked for a disabled permit on your car, but I couldn't find one.

Woman: What's it to you?

You: I *do* have a permit but found no designated spot available.

Woman: Not my problem.

You: You are saying that you have no permit?

Woman: I don't have to talk to you.

You: True. However, you may want to have a talk with your conscience. It will tell you that taking one of these spots when you are not disabled is wrong. Next time, please do the right thing.

~

THE CIVIL DRIVER

If everyone photocopied this list and placed it on the windshields of cars whose drivers have engaged in rude behavior, we could make a big dent (!) in the lack of civility on our roads.

- Be alert.
- Know and observe speed limits.
- Always signal your turns.
- Brake and stop gradually.
- Change to the appropriate lane far in advance of an exit ramp or turn.
- Avoid using bright headlights if any cars are heading toward you.
- Stop fully at stop signs.
- Don't try to run red lights.
- Look carefully in every direction when leaving a parking space.

- Don't use your horn unless absolutely necessary.
- Allow cars to merge in front of you easily.
- No matter how small the collision, stop and check if you have damaged the other car in any way.
- Leave a note with your contact information if you damage a parked car whose owner is somewhere else.
- Unless you are disabled, never, ever park in a handicapped parking spot.

THE SITUATION. *Someone Cuts in Line Just Ahead of You.* The person behind you in the roped lane at airport security has been gaining ground so that she is now beside you. At the next turn of the line, she nonchalantly tries to pull ahead. It's time to speak up with firm composure.

THE SOLUTION. Say: "Excuse me, I believe you are behind me." If the other person ignores you, you may add: "Ma'am, please keep to your place in line." If even this brings no positive result, you will have to stop so that the incident doesn't escalate.

THE SITUATION. *On a Plane, a Fellow Passenger Is Exceedingly Chatty.* You are sitting on a plane next to someone who overestimates your interest in the details of his or her life. The flow of words is relentless, and you are a captive audience. You would much prefer to read a book or revise a document on your computer but are reluctant to speak up for fear of being discourteous.

THE SOLUTION. It is your trip, and it is your time. You are entitled to peace and quiet and fully justified in saying: "If you don't mind, I would like to take a break from our conversation now. It's going to be a long day, and I need to relax and collect my thoughts." *Break* is a good word here because it sounds temporary rather than dismissive, and you may not mind exchanging a few courtesy words later, just before landing. Try not to feel bad about expressing your need. You are not doing anything wrong; you are just being a good steward of your mental and physical resources.

⁓

THE SITUATION. *On a Plane, Fellow Passengers Hog the Armrests.* The two passengers seated at your sides act as though they own the armrests you are supposed to share. You feel cramped in your middle seat and would like very much to enjoy those extra inches.

THE SOLUTION. When it looks like your turn to stretch is not coming any time soon, say: "Please, allow me to rest my arm now. Shall we take turns using the armrest for the duration of the flight?"

⁓

THE SITUATION. *On a Plane, a Fellow Passenger Invades Your Space.* You are trying to relax during a very long flight. The passenger sitting behind you keeps going to the bathroom. Every time, she yanks the back of your seat to pull herself out of hers as she steps into the aisle. She seems oblivious to any annoyance this might cause you. You finally get tired of being shaken.

THE SOLUTION. Explain how you are inconvenienced and request a change like this: "Excuse me, but I am trying to rest. Your shaking the back of my seat really doesn't help." "And how am I supposed to get up from *my* seat?" is a likely response, which will find you ready to respond in turn: "If you push up on your armrests, you won't need to pull on my seat."

⁓

THE SITUATION. *On a Plane, Parents Don't Make an Effort to Keep Their Child Quiet.* Ever since the flight started, ear-piercing shrieks from an overstimulated and fussy two-year-old have tried your patience. His parents do not seem interested in calming him down. In fact, they keep engaging him in a mild form of roughhousing that has the opposite effect.

THE SOLUTION. First, ask a flight attendant to bring the issue of other passengers' tranquillity to the parents' attention. If this does not yield the hoped-for result, you may want to try your luck with the parents yourself. But be prepared for a hostile reaction.

> You: Excuse me, we have a long trip ahead of us. Would you please try to keep your child quiet?
>
> Mother: How do you suppose I can do that? Do you want me to put a pillow over his face?
>
> You: No, I'm just asking you to make an effort to quiet him. If he remains at this level of excitement, it will be next to impossible for other people to relax and rest.

⌒

THE SITUATION. *On a Plane, Parents Ignore Their Child Kicking Your Seat.* The restless child behind you keeps kicking the back of your seat.

THE SOLUTION. Say to the adult in charge: "Excuse me, you may not be aware that your child is kicking the back of my seat. Would you make sure that she doesn't? I really would like to relax." This is a formula that combines courtesy and determination. The adult in question probably understands that you will pursue the matter until you are satisfied. It is always possible, however, that you will have to take your complaint to your flight attendant, who may arrange a change of seats. Who knows? If you are really lucky, they might even upgrade you.

THE SITUATION. *A Flight Attendant Snaps at You.* As the flight attendant is about to hand you the cup of water, you inform her: "We already got our water, thank you." "That's because you rang twice," the flight attendant sharply replies. "Do not do that. It drives us crazy when people do that." And off she goes in a huff. "So much for customer service!" you can't help thinking.

THE SOLUTION. At the first moment of calm between service runs, look for the flight attendant and tell her you would like to apologize. "I'm sorry. Your colleague brought me the water a moment after I rang again. I should have been a little more patient." Then address the issue of her edgy reaction: "I wish you had just informed me that for whatever reason it can take you five or more minutes to answer a call. Being scolded certainly made me feel young, but it felt a little excessive too." This will give her the opportunity to apologize in turn.

THE SITUATION. *Someone Asks Your Permission to Cut in Line.* As you wait your turn to purchase a train ticket, someone rushing from the concourse asks if he can cut in front of you since his train is leaving in five minutes.

THE SOLUTION. Reply: "I'm sorry, but as you can see I am not the only one here. I can't speak for everybody behind me. It's their time too. They may also have trains that leave in the next five or ten minutes. I'm afraid you need to go to the end of the line."

THE SITUATION. *A Loud Passenger Spoils the Quiet in the Quiet Car.* Having chosen to sit in your train's quiet car, you look forward to a couple of hours of undisturbed reading. No sooner has the conductor explained the quiet car rules over the PA system, however, than an irritating ringtone pierces the silence. It is the woman sitting beside you who answers it, to give a very loud and detailed report of the rush-hour taxi ride that took her to the train station. This call is immediately followed by another, just as loud.

THE SOLUTION. Since the conductor is not around, you decide to remind the caller that this is a quiet car and telephone calls are not allowed. The issue-evading response "What are you, the noise police?" is de rigueur. Remaining calm and collected, simply respond: "No, I am just someone expecting quiet in the quiet car." By the time she counters with the blame-shifting "You surely are making a big deal out of this. Why don't you lighten up a little?" it is time to stop unilaterally what is starting to sound like a squabble. Hope that from now on she will follow the rules. If the disturbance continues, look for the conductor.

~

THE SITUATION. *A Passenger Is Occupying Two Seats on a Crowded Train.* A young man is asleep stretched over two seats. When you wake him up politely, claiming a seat for yourself, he looks at you askance, huffs, and mumbles something that sounds like "I'm sleeping here. Grab another seat."

THE SOLUTION. Say: "There *are* no other seats. Your ticket entitles you to one seat, not two. I have a ticket also, but no seat yet. I am sorry to have to ask, but I *am* asking." If he refuses to comply, see the conductor.

~

THE SITUATION. *Fellow Train Passengers Keep Cursing in Front of Your Child.* On a commuter train with your seven-year-old daughter, you are sitting across from a young man and a young woman. Wearing T-shirts with college insignias, they punctuate their conversation with profanities that you find distasteful and disturbing. You hope that they will adjust their language to the situation, but they don't.

THE SOLUTION. Say: "Excuse me, may I ask you to skip the profanities? I find them offensive, and I don't want my child exposed to them. I wish I didn't have to ask you, but as you see there is no privacy here." Of course, the youngsters may respond with a particularly stinging curse and ignore your request. At that point you can talk to the conductor or look for other seats.

9. The World of Service

Does poor service drive customers to behave rudely? Yes. Is customer rudeness responsible for poor service? Yes. Breaking this vicious circle is a worthwhile goal for any of us who shop in stores, eat in restaurants, go to doctors, answer the telephone—in other words, live in this world.

What causes the vicious circle, though? Say your job is to serve me my meal. I may see you only in relation to that, as if you were just a convenient robot—shuttling dishes to and from the kitchen—completely overlooking you as an individual human being. Are you tired? Are you hot in your uniform? Do you have a sick child? I don't ask myself these questions. You are the function you are performing for me. Needless to say, civility doesn't blossom easily in this soil. Just as plenty of customers have little regard for service workers, many service workers treat their customers with indifference or even contempt. There is a residue of stigma attached to service—especially certain kinds—that harks back to the times when servants performed it. In part because of this, service workers often see their jobs as unappealing and unrewarding. Neither customers nor service workers find it easy to be purposefully, considerately, and positively engaged.

Then, there is the fact that money is being exchanged. For most of us, spending is difficult. It may even feel a little traumatic. We may like to shop and buy, but we experience parting with our money as a loss. As we give it up, we feel unsettled, vulnerable, and unconsciously resentful toward the salesperson taking it from us. I doubt this basic psychology is taught to service workers. It should be, because it helps explain why it doesn't take much for people spending money to feel victimized and snarl back. Ironically, it is when anger enters the picture that the relationship becomes personal.

In this chapter I focus on customers responding to service provider rudeness because service providers' response to customer rudeness is often a matter of company policy. For a brief review of the basic principles that apply in the latter situation, however, see the box on page 147.

THE SITUATION. *A Salesperson Ignores You.* Your salesperson is engaged in a personal telephone call, devotes more time than necessary to the customer ahead of you, or is conversing with a coworker.

THE SOLUTION. Say: "Excuse me, I just want to make sure you saw me. I have been waiting for the last ten minutes." If you are told to wait your turn, say: "I was not sure I was waiting my turn, because nobody acknowledged I was here." This ought to speed things up. If, instead, the exchange turns argumentative, bring it to an end: "I think I will look for help elsewhere." And that can mean looking for another salesperson, involving a supervisor, or taking your business to the competition.

~

THE SITUATION. *A Phone Customer Receives Precedence over You.* At your favorite department store, you've spent a couple of hours choosing a new winter coat and then waited in line quite a long time to pay for it. You are about to hand the coat to the salesperson at the register when he asks you to wait a moment as he takes a telephone call. You feel as though someone has been allowed to cut in front of you in line. The calling customer, who has a complicated question, is receiving plenty of attention. You also soon realize it's not going to be just a moment's wait. Although you are tempted to leave right then and there, you decide not to.

THE SOLUTION. Once the call ends, be ready to express your displeasure.

You: Do you always give precedence to customers on the phone?

Salesperson: What else can we do?

You: Having another employee answer the calls is one possible solution. Another is to tell the caller that there is someone in line before them, that you will put them on hold and be back on the line when it's their turn.

Salesperson: We would lose a lot of business that way.

You: Maybe, until people realize that it's only fair. What you do now punishes the customer who has made the effort to come to your store. I was about to leave. You risked losing my business too.

⌒

THE SITUATION. *Your Salesperson's Attitude Is Not What You Expect.* You are dealing with a salesperson whose attitude is disengaged, uncooperative, condescending, or surly. The feeling that you are being taken for granted bothers you. You expect to be accorded a higher standard of professional courtesy.

THE SOLUTION. Say: "Excuse me, I may be mistaken, but you seem to be having a bad day. May I help?" The salesperson will hardly believe his ears. Here is a client who is not demanding help but offering it. Don't be surprised if you end up receiving particularly good service.

⤬

THE SITUATION. *A Simple Purchase Turns into a Disclosure of Your Personal Data.* As you pay for your purchase, you are asked for your name, address, telephone number, or zip code. While the salesperson makes it sound as though you *must* give that information, you know better and resent the little game. You are also acutely aware that little privacy is left in the digital age and do not want to divulge casually personal information.

THE SOLUTION. Don't confront the salesperson, asking him or her how it feels to aid and abet corporate duplicity; likewise, don't provide false information as a form of protest. Just say: "I don't give that out," "It's unlisted," or "I prefer not to." You may choose to add: "You may want to let your customers know that they don't *have* to disclose that information."

⤬

THE SITUATION. *Your Salesperson Does Not Respect Your Privacy.* A salesperson introduces himself to you and your husband, thrusting out his right hand and demanding to know your names. You feel that ordinary business transactions can be happily conducted in mutual, polite ignorance of personal identity. He is the representative of his firm, and you are the customer entrusted to his care. That's all.

THE SOLUTION. You want your exchange to go like this:

Salesperson: Hi, I'm Les. And what is your name?

You: Ma'am.

Salesperson: Excuse me?

You: You can call me Ma'am. Thank you.

This should suffice. Facing a persistently intrusive employee, however, you may want to point out that when you shop you enjoy being just a client and you treasure your privacy.

⌁

THE SITUATION. *You Are Stuck with an Overzealous Waitress.* You and your fellow diners have taken only a couple of sips from your wineglasses when your waitress hastens to refill them. She then immediately refills your water glasses with mineral water. From a previous visit you know that she will continue to do so throughout the meal. You have two problems with this. First, you believe that, as a blatant attempt to increase consumption, her service crosses the boundary between prompt and pushy. Second, you know that it favors the inconsiderate drinker in your party who quickly empties his or her glass.

THE SOLUTION. Thinking "This is our table and these are our beverages," you take charge. After the first refill, tell your waitress: "Thank you. From now on we'll take care of the pouring ourselves." Or tell her you'll let her know when it's time to pour. A word of caution: The first option may be considered improper because you take over her task. The second appears to be a good compromise. It is she who at this point may ask you if you prefer to pour your own wine.

～

THE SITUATION. *A Restaurant Fails a Hygiene Test.* While in a restaurant's restroom, you notice the waiter who just took your order. Although he is coming out of a stall and buckling his belt, there are no accompanying flushing noises. Also, showing no inclination to stop at the sinks first, he heads for the door. All of a sudden your appetite is less robust. What to do? Pretend that you did not see anything? Tell the maître d' you have changed your mind about dinner and are leaving? Your meal would probably be spoiled if you were served by that waiter. Furthermore, you feel you should disclose the hygiene breach for the sake of fellow and future diners.

THE SOLUTION. Tell the manager that you are not comfortable being served by someone who fails to observe elementary rules of personal hygiene. You now have the choice of leaving or asking to be served by a different waiter.

～

THE SITUATION. *You Receive Very Inadequate Restaurant Service.* At the end of an expensive restaurant meal, you feel that your waiter's performance was very disappointing. Twenty-five minutes went by before he came to collect your beverage order. He eventually brought wine, although not the one you ordered, and designer mineral water, which you definitely did *not* order. The much-coveted bread basket never made it to your table. He neither explained nor apologized for the long delays in delivery of each course. Your inquiries about the fate of your food brought dismissive replies. You would have liked to take a look at the dessert menu, but when he brought you your check without waiting for you to ask, you decided you had had enough.

THE SOLUTION. Explain to the restaurant manager that the service you received substantially reduced your enjoyment of your meal and for this reason you are leaving a smaller tip or no tip at all.

THE SITUATION. *You Are Made to Wait an Unreasonably Long Time at Your Doctor's Office.* Your scheduled time to see Dr. Roselli was an hour ago. The clipboard-toting nurse calling the patients' names has disappeared, and the administrative assistant has ignored you all along. You can't believe that nobody explained to you the reason for the delay or apologized for it. Actually you can, your customer service expectations being what they are. This is still not right, however. Your time is valuable too.

THE SOLUTION. Walk to the administrative assistant's counter, inform her that your appointment was an hour ago, and ask when you can expect to be summoned. If she barely lifts her head as she curtly tells you that you will be called when it's your turn, say: "I'm afraid that doesn't answer my question. Having been waiting for the past sixty minutes, I feel entitled to an estimate of when I may actually get to see the doctor. This is a workday for me as well, and I have commitments to keep. Please find out from Dr. Roselli, if necessary."

When you finally get to see the doctor, say: "Dr. Roselli, I trust you as a doctor and I like you as a person. I want you to continue as my physician. However, please understand that I need to rely on your punctuality. I sit in your waiting room an average of thirty or forty minutes every time I come here. No one ever offers explanations or apologies. On the days I see you, I have to schedule work appointments too. I need you and your office to be mindful of the value of my time."

THE SITUATION. *You Receive a Dinnertime Solicitation via Telephone.* Here it comes, yet another dinnertime telephone call from someone who wants you (1) to contribute to a worthy charitable cause or (2) to take advantage of a deal you can't pass up.

THE SOLUTION. (1) If you have no intention of making a donation, say: "I am sorry, but I am not adding new organizations to my charity list" or "I'm sorry, this time I am not contributing." If the caller insists, you insist as well: "No, thank you, my decision is final." (2) If you have no intention to buy and also resent the invasion of your privacy, say: "Allow me to interrupt you so that we don't waste each other's time. I am not interested in your product. Also, I don't do my shopping at dinnertime. Please make sure you put my name on your don't call list." Then add, "Thank you, have a good day."

⁓

THE SITUATION. *You Receive a Smart-Alecky Reply.* Knowing that you need electrical work done in your office, a savvy colleague tells you to ask for Ron at Plant Operations. When you call, the woman on the phone tells you that Ron is on sick leave and won't be back for the rest of the week. "May I talk to you?" you say then. Her reply is "Why do you think I'm answering?" You resent her implication that it was silly or wrong of you to ask the question.

THE SOLUTION. The response "Never mind. On second thought, I'll wait until Ron returns" is not the most polite of options. Letting the slight go unnoticed and just mentioning your problem is too self-effacing. The preferable option is an explanation: "I asked because I did not know if listening to my problem was part of your job or if you redirected Ron's calls to his voice mail."

Few jobs are as challenging as those requiring a lot of direct contact with customers. The challenge is particularly arduous when the customer is angry. Here is a tipsheet on how to deal with it professionally and effectively.

HOW TO DEAL WITH AN
ANGRY CUSTOMER

1. **Understand Your Customer's Anger.** Anger is a legitimate feeling. Accept that your customer is angry and assume that his or her anger is not groundless. Respond with empathy but in a businesslike manner. Keep some distance from what is happening, to remain clearheaded. If it helps, imagine that you are being videotaped and that your taped interaction will be used to train new employees at your company.

2. **Interruptions Don't Help.** Do not interrupt your customer. Carefully separate in your mind the reason for the anger from the angry tone and consider the merit of the complaint. Do not preach or chastise. Your task is to solve a problem, not to reform character. When the customer has finished speaking, say: "I understand," "I see how this can be frustrating," "I'm sorry to hear that," or "Let me try something."

3. **Remain Engaged and in Control.** Do not say, "I don't know," "It's not my department," or "There is nothing I can do." Say instead: "I'll be glad to help you," "I can find out for you," or "Let me try something else." If appropriate, offer to call your supervisor.

4. **Empathize.** When facing a protracted complaint, reiterate your expressions of empathy: "I *do* see your point." "You *are* entitled to an answer." When facing an outburst, state with poise that yelling won't help: "Sir, I need you to calm down so that we can work together on this." "Ma'am, please help me find a solution that is acceptable to you." Establish a mood of collaboration.

5. **Remember, This Is Business.** Do not take your customer's angry words personally. Remember, you just happen to be in the

(continued)

line of fire. Had you been on vacation today, someone else would be in your place now. To keep the exchange from becoming personal, visualize some entity other than you (your company or your customer's personal-life frustrations) as the cause of your customer's anger. Give your name if your customer asks for it.

6. **Keep Your Composure**. Do not belittle your customer's complaints, and do not use sarcasm or profanities. Never respond to a customer's outburst with one of your own. If your customer's anger escalates to dangerous levels, call a time-out: "Ma'am, I believe that we both need to step back from this. Let me see if someone can help us." Summoning a supervisor or security officer is a good option if you become the target of abuse or threats.

7. **Smile.** A sincere, cordial smile at the appropriate moment has been known to defuse many a tense exchange. A smile makes the customer feel treated like an individual, not an anonymous and faceless entity.

10. Digital Communication

PEOPLE SAY AND DO THINGS IN CYBERSPACE THAT THEY
WOULDN'T ORDINARILY SAY AND DO IN THE FACE-TO-FACE
WORLD.

—John Suler

THE HELL WITH CIVILITY. CIVILITY IS FOR FACE TO FACE. THE
INTERNET COMMENT IS FOR SAYING WHAT YOU REALLY FEEL.

—yourboytony

Many see the opportunity afforded by our access to cyberspace to communicate freely, easily, and inexpensively with the whole world as a triumph of democracy. Others fear that the Internet might shape our lives for the worse in ways that will become completely clear only with the passing of time. Either way, it's clear that online communication has unleashed a new magnitude of rudeness. The virtual world allows us to vent our hostility without revealing our identities. Anonymity makes millions of us digital snipers. To paraphrase Odysseus's words to the Cyclops, "Our name is Nobody." We are Nobodies communicating with Nobodies. Snideness is the order of the day.

Even when we communicate with people we know, we are less restrained because we don't have to deal with their reactions the way we would if they were present (even as a voice on the phone). Thinking about what happens online as not "really real," but rather as taking place in an alternate reality, gives many of us further license for abuse. This is when life feels like a video game, where everybody gets hit but nobody gets hurt. Whatever the reasons might be, millions of digital denizens believe that (or at least act as though) on the Net anything can be said about anybody and to anybody at any time. The digital world seems to have become a repository of our collective moral toxins. What happens on the Net, however, does not stay on the Net. The "everything goes" mode of online communication is inevitably causing a relaxing of standards in the offline world.

THE SITUATION. *You Receive a Rude E-Mail.* Here it is: a rude e-mail in which a co-worker accuses you in not so many words of being ungrateful and duplicitous. Angry and resentful, for a moment all you think about is evening the score with a blistering reply. Clicking "Send" is going to feel so good. Or is it?

THE SOLUTION. Maybe it *will* feel good, but not for long. Responding to rudeness with rudeness leaves a bitter taste in the mouths of decent people. Before composing and firing off your hostile message, stop and think. Once you click, there is no unclicking. Have you considered that you might be overreacting? What you want to avoid is a full-blown e-mail altercation. In its wake, any relationship you might have with the other person will never be the same. Also, your angry messages can come back to haunt you as they reach eyes for which they were not intended. Ostensibly about the character of the other person, they will also reveal your own. Not responding—at least for now—may be the wisest response.

Take time to cool off. Reread the message: Does its tone strike you as less offensive now? The absence of gesture and voice cues makes e-mail statements more difficult to interpret than statements uttered in physical presence or even on the telephone. Also, you now realize that your co-worker may be basing her displeasure upon an incorrect version of the facts in question. After calming down, write: "Deborah, I wish to make sure I understood your position in the e-mail you sent me earlier today. What, exactly, is it that makes you unhappy, and what were you told happened in the meeting?"

THE SITUATION. *An E-Mail Message Makes You Uncomfortable.* Your friend Ken either considers e-mail secure or does not care who might have access to his messages—his choice of topics and the language he uses make that very clear. Lately, Ken has been sending you e-mails about your sister, who has been in and out of rehab. He thinks he's showing concern by asking about her and providing referrals, but you know that nothing is private online and prefer to keep sensitive information from reaching unintended interested parties.

THE SOLUTION. Call Ken, tell him that you are not comfortable with his messages, explain why ("I consider this a matter for Jennifer to address if she chooses to"), and inform him that you don't wish to receive such messages again. Add any other topics (politics, sex?) you will not discuss online and make it clear that you expect him to comply with your preferences.

THE SITUATION. *Someone Improperly Handles Your E-Mail.* You discover that your friend has posted on her community affairs blog a personal e-mail of yours without asking for your permission. You tell yourself that your message, which was about your opposition to artificial turf for local soccer fields, does not contain anything that could damage you, but you are still bothered by your friend's cavalier attitude. You want to prevent her from doing this in the future.

THE SOLUTION. Call your friend and impress upon her that you want to communicate only with her, not with the entire world. You want her to ask your permission whenever she wishes to use what you wrote.

THE SITUATION. *Someone Else Improperly Handles Your E-Mail.* Stan, your second in command, was fiercely loyal to the department head you replaced only months ago. Now it comes to your attention that he has been forwarding e-mails of yours to colleagues and even to his retired boss without your authorization and appending the occasional snide comment.

THE SOLUTION. Call a meeting with him and say: "Stan, I know that you had great admiration for Steve, but now I am in charge, and I need your unequivocal support. My job is tough as it is without internal sniping. Unless I specify differently, my e-mails are not to be divulged in any way. If you have problems with them, I'm here. Steve is not coming back, and the company must move on. I hope that you are onboard." Consider putting in place a policy forbidding the forwarding outside the company of intracompany e-mail.

THE SITUATION. *Friends Send You Too Much E-Mail.* A good friend of yours keeps sending you spam, news stories, links to blogs, jokes, inspirational quotes, chain-mail messages, lists of all kinds, et cetera. Some of the material is interesting, some is digital flotsam. You do not have time to sift through it, and your friend expects you to respond to each item. She then selects preferred items for exhaustive e-mail conversation, clearly expressing disappointment if you demur. Increasingly ill at ease, you consider your options.

THE SOLUTION. Humoring her with the occasional response will not satisfy her and will still be a burden to you. Just ignoring her messages strikes you as rude and would certainly hurt her feelings. It's time to send a thoughtful e-mail. "Leslie, I appreciate your wanting to share with me your Internet finds. Unfortunately, things are so busy at work and at home these days that I simply don't have the time to read and respond. I'm sorry. I very much look forward to our upcoming last-Friday-of-the-month lunch."

⁓

THE SITUATION. *Your Spouse Is Too Connected.* An accomplished and driven businessman, your husband checks his Black-Berry compulsively both during dinners at home and when the family eats out (weekends included). You find this ungracious, uncaring, and an altogether bad example for the children.

THE SOLUTION. Stipulate that the use of digital gadgets is banned during meals and explain the reason to your children: We owe one another the gift of full presence. When we communicate electronically with the wide world, we are only half-present for those with whom we share physical space here and now. We don't do full justice to our being together.

⁓

THE SITUATION. *Your Colleagues Are Too Connected.* Several of the colleagues you supervise answer their cell phones or work on their e-mail while they are in meetings. You find the practice distracting, annoying, and unprofessional.

THE SOLUTION. Tell your colleagues—tactfully—that out of respect for all involved, including the clients who while not present are still interested parties, you hope they will set their digital devices aside and give their full attention to the matters at hand. Point out that banning digital distraction may even result in shorter meetings.

⁓

THE SITUATION. *A Guest Hogs the Computer in the Hotel's Business Center.* The hotel where you are staying is small, and its minuscule business center has only one computer with an Internet connection. You would like to check your e-mail, but another guest has been sitting in front of the screen for some time. When you return from breakfast and find that the same person is still using the terminal, you decide to speak up.

THE SOLUTION. Say: "Excuse me, would you mind letting me take a turn at the computer? There is only one for all the guests, and I really need to check my e-mail before I begin my workday." If the computer-hogging guest ignores your plea for fair use, your only alternative to giving up is requesting the intervention of the shift manager.

⁓

THE SITUATION. *A Stranger Wants to Borrow Your Computer.* Sitting in the airport waiting lounge and realizing you still have fifty minutes before boarding time, you decide to do some work on your laptop. A few minutes later the passenger seated next to you asks if you would mind letting him check his e-mail on your computer. While you don't like the sound of that request, you don't want to appear discourteous. For a moment the latter concern seems to prevail, but in the end you decide that you don't *have* to do something you really don't *want* to.

THE SOLUTION. Say: "I'm sorry, but I am not comfortable letting others use my computer. Have you noticed if the airport has a travelers' business center?"

～

THE SITUATION. *People Fail to Respect Your Privacy.* A colleague casts curious glances over your shoulder at your computer screen every time he comes to your cubicle. A stranger sitting beside you on a plane seems very interested in the e-mail you are checking on your laptop. They may have no malicious intention, but what they are doing is rude, and you have reason to be annoyed.

THE SOLUTION. Asking "Is there something you are looking for?" or "May I help you find something?" should dissuade them. Only the most brazen snoops will require an explicit prohibition such as "Excuse me, but I consider what I have in my computer to be personal until I decide to divulge it. I hope you'll respect that."

～

THE SITUATION. *A Colleague Needs to Show More Respect to Your Staff.* Gerry, who travels for your company a lot, regularly e-mails his expense reports to Amy, part of whose job it is to process them. Gerry, however, also CCs the reports to you, Amy's boss. Although Amy has never made an issue of it, you believe that Gerry's involving you can be construed as a slight to her—as though he weren't comfortable trusting just her with his reports.

THE SOLUTION. E-mail Gerry, saying something like "Gerry, although I appreciate your thoroughness, please note that there is no need to CC me when you e-mail Amy. She is the one in charge of the ordinary processing of reports. Being competent and reliable, she deserves full credit for her job."

～

THE SITUATION. *A Business Associate Needs a Basic Course in E-Mail Etiquette.* A valuable business associate of yours, Gordon is competent, bright, and reliable. Unfortunately, he is a messy e-mailer, and since e-mail is the main means of communication between the two of you, this is a problem. After making allowances for a while, you come to the conclusion that he needs to receive an explicit e-mail on the topic of e-mail.

THE SOLUTION. Write: "Gordon, my friend, I need your help here. We exchange so much e-mail that I must ask you to pay attention to a couple of things to make my life easier. Do fill in the subject line every time, so that I can better prioritize the opening of my messages and also be reminded of their contents later without having to open them again. If you use the reply function, do not mess with the original message, so that I can refer to it to refresh my memory. And finally, please, please check your messages for spelling and grammar. Although it does take me more time to understand unrevised messages, the main reason I'm asking is that I often need to forward your e-mails to people who frown upon such an informal way of communicating. If you don't clean them up, I have to. Thank you very much for understanding."

~

THE SITUATION. *A Chat Group Member Creates a Problem.* In your chat group of Latin music lovers, Emily is known for expressing her opinions without mincing words. Usually nobody seems to mind, but one day she criticizes the group's favorite singer's handling of his private life. That is when you receive an e-mail from Jessica, another group member, who argues that being unsupportive of her idol makes Emily unfit to continue as a group member. With the good of the group foremost in mind, you wonder how to craft your response to an underhanded strategy that you find objectionable.

THE SOLUTION. Write: "Dear Jessica, I think that in all fairness your message should be posted on the board for everybody to see, just as Emily posted hers. As an alternative, you could e-mail it to her, since it is about her. Allow me to put it back in your hands then, so that you can decide what you want to do with it. All I know is that Emily has been a very active and loyal member of our group for the last two years and that I have great respect for her."

~

THE SITUATION. *An Unwelcome E-Mailer Emerges from Your Past.* Rich, a friend from your distant past, e-mails you out of the blue, intent on reclaiming a place of some kind in your life. You, by contrast, are ill at ease. After years of silence, you perceive these advances as intrusive. As you respond with polite e-mails that become less frequent and shorter, you never address your displeasure explicitly, hoping that your correspondent will understand and desist. He doesn't. Sometimes you figure you'll keep responding, because "after all he doesn't mean any harm." And sometimes you feel like sending a terse e-mail saying that he is a pestering nuisance.

THE SOLUTION. Honest without being dismissive and forceful without being hostile: This is what you want to be as you write the farewell message. "Rich, so much has happened to both of us since we were last in touch! Not only did we live separate lives, but I feel that we have become different persons as well. I am sorry, but I must tell you that I am not ready to reconnect. I know you will understand my wish to concentrate on my life today. Going back to another time and another me just does not feel like something I need right now. Good-bye from your old friend, and plenty of happiness to you and yours."

Although tactfully crafted, this is still a rejection and as such may elicit a bitter and even angry reply ("I can't believe . . . I thought we were friends . . . You are full of yourself . . . What a mistake it was to write . . . I didn't deserve . . ."). You may respond very simply: "I am sorry you feel like that, but it doesn't change how I feel." The alternative—a good one—is silence.

Closing Thoughts

RELATIONSHIPS ARE THE FOUNDATION OF HUMANITY. WE DE-
RIVE OUR NOURISHMENT FROM THEM, LEARN FROM THEM, AND
THRIVE THROUGH THEM. EVERY HUMAN BEING WANTS TO RE-
LATE TO OTHER HUMAN BEINGS; IT IS AN ESSENTIAL PART OF
WHO WE ARE AS INDIVIDUALS AND AS A SPECIES. AND THE WAY
IN WHICH WE RELATE TO OTHERS DETERMINES HOW HAPPY
WE ARE, HOW LONG WE LIVE, AND THE CHOICES WE MAKE.
THROUGH OUR RELATIONSHIPS WE DISCOVER OUR PLACE IN THE
WORLD AND OUR REASON FOR BEING HERE.

—*Christopher Hansard*

In closing, I am going to turn to my friend, psychologist Arthur
Ciaramicoli. His tipsheet, which you will find below, is as good a
summary as any of the main points of this book. It pleases me to
bring my work to completion with the help of words of wisdom that
place emphasis on the role of empathy in dealing with rudeness.

1. Don't personalize rude behavior—it's unlikely to be about
   you although it's directed to you.
2. Be aware that rude behavior comes from various sources
   (i.e., sleep deprivation, depression, stress, illness, insecurity,
   et cetera).

3. Respond with calmness rather than behavior that escalates rude behavior.

4. "An eye for an eye" is a poor approach; don't buy another's insecurity and make it your own.

5. Self-righteous behavior only reflects poorly on you; don't use the opportunity to demean another.

6. Try to address the underlying cause of the behavior ("I can see you are very stressed. Maybe I could help if you tell me what's bothering you").

7. When necessary, set limits tactfully and assertively, not aggressively.

8. If the conversation remains irrational, know when to quit.

9. Don't assume rudeness is a permanent part of someone's personality. It is a pattern of rudeness that determines character not one mishap.

10. In the end, always let empathy—the ability to read others accurately—be your guide in understanding rudeness, knowing how to respond to a rude individual and knowing when to leave the scene.

A final thought. Someone was rude to you, you were hurt, but you responded in a temperate, assertive, and overall effective way. Maybe the other person proffered an apology. What now? Forgiving is next. By granting forgiveness, you come to terms with what happened, obtain closure, and thus find yourself better equipped to go on with your life. Forgiving (which, like gratitude, is a form of acceptance) has a healing effect not only on you but also on the person who hurt you and in the process hurt him- or herself. It creates an eleventh-hour bond that can keep your relationship alive. Apologies and forgiveness are the lifesavers of relationships. They are two splendid examples of smart ways of treating others well. Use them unsparingly as you go through the wonderful and difficult experience in relating and connecting that we call life.

Notes

I am grateful to my friend Marci Treece, who wrote me about her rude encounter and allowed me to share it with my readers. Her story appears here in a shorter and minimally edited version. I have preserved both its main features and its details.

Never let rudeness catch you. For a crash course on responding to rudeness, see Peggy Post, *Emily Post's Etiquette* (New York: HarperResource, 2004), pp. 35–42.

1. On Rudeness

5 **Opinion surveys have been reporting.** See the much-quoted 1996 U.S. News/Bozell survey (http://www.unc.edu/courses/ 2007spring/poli/055/001/Readings/Apr%205/Civility%20Quality %20Quotient.htm). It was on this data that John Marks based his story "The American Uncivil Wars," which appeared in *U.S. News & World Report,* April 22, 1996, pp. 66–72. For more recent data, see the survey "Aggravating Circumstances: A Status Report on Rudeness in America," prepared by Public Agenda for the Pew Charitable Trusts and dated 2002 (http://www.publicagenda.org/ press/press_release_detail.cfm?report_title-Aggravating%20Cir-cumstances). Also of interest are the Associated Press–Ipsos survey

of 2005 (www.usatoday.com/news/nation/2005-10-14-rudeness-poll-method_x.htm) and the ABC News *20/20* survey of 2006 as reported by Jon Cohen and Gary Langer, in "Poll-Rudeness in America, 2006," abcnews.go.com/ 2020/US/story?id=1574155.

15 **Duly Noted: The Cost of Rudeness.** For the people issues figure, see ComPsych's StressPulse survey of 2006 (http://www.compsych.com/jsp/en_US/content/pressRelease/2006/coworkerConflict.jsp). For the other figure, and a wealth of enlightening information, see the website of the American Institute of Stress (www.stress.org).

15 **Ninety percent of American workers.** See the studies by Christine Porath at the University of Southern California as reported by Loretta Chao in "Rise in Office Rudeness Weighs on Productivity and Retention," can be found at www.careerjournal.com/hrcenter/articles/20060119-chao.html.

15 **One study's estimate.** See the Accountemps-ICR study on workplace conflict as reported by Jan H. Kennedy, in "Conundrums Co-Workers Face," at www.icrsurvey.com/Study.aspx?f=Accountemps%20-%20Conundrums%20co-workers%20Face%2011-26-06.htm.

15 **We know for a fact.** See, for instance, Shaoni Bhattacharya, "Unfair Bosses Make Blood Pressure Soar," http://www.newscientist.com/article.ns?id=dn3863.

16 **A 2006 survey reported.** See "Poor Customer Service Drives Nearly Half of U.S. Consumers to Take Their Business Elsewhere, Accenture Survey Finds," http://accenture.tekgroup.com/article_display.cfm?article_id=4394.

16 **To give salespeople their due.** All other things being equal, a substantial and indeed often decisive advantage goes to companies

that are managed as though they were in the business of building relationships. Workers with good relational skills are a major factor in gaining and maintaining customer loyalty. When service is rude, business suffers because clients are unhappy. When business suffers, service is rude because service providers are unhappy. When service is civil, business thrives because clients are happy. When business thrives, service is more civil because service providers are happy.

19 **In 2006 about two-thirds.** See David Crary, "It's All About Me," http://findarticles.com/p/articles/mi-qn4155/is_20070227/ai_n18635946.

20 **As Tim Kasser documents.** See Tim Kasser, *The High Price of Materialism* (Cambridge, Mass., and London, England: MIT Press, 2003), pp. 61–72.

22 **One-third of employed Americans.** See the 2005 study "Overwork in America: When the Way We Work Becomes Too Much," by the Families and Work Institute, as reported in "New Study Reveals One in Three Americans Are Chronically Overworked," http://familiesandwork.org/site/newsroom/releases/2005overwork .html.

22 ***Newsweek* magazine reported.** See Herbert Benson, Julie Colliss, Geoffrey Cowley, "Brain Check," September 27, 2004, p. 47.

23 **When it came to identifying.** See the Associated Press–Ipsos survey of 2005, www.usatoday.com/news/nation/2005-10-14-rudeness-poll -method_x.htm.

23 **Duly Noted: Bus Uncle's Rudeness.** See Geoffrey A. Fowler, "A Six-Minute Tirade on a Hong Kong Bus Rides into Vernacular," http://online.wsj.com/article/SB114962497534572979.htm

2. PREVENTING RUDENESS

45 **A person more likable.** On the topic, see Tim Sanders, *The Likeability Factor* (New York: Crown, 2005).

46 **Set the mood.** "And as I watched him operate, I noticed that he always acted as if the other fellow's friendly response was a foregone conclusion. Because he *believed* other people would like him, he *acted as if* they would like him....*He Assumed the Attitude He Expected the Other Person to Take.*" Les Giblin, *How to Have Confidence & Power in Dealing with People* (New York: Barnes & Noble, 1999), p. 71.

47 **Andrew J. DuBrin**. See his excellent manual, *Human Relations: Interpersonal Job-Oriented Skills*, 9th ed. (Upper Saddle River, NJ: Pearson Prentice-Hall, 2007), pp. 22–23.

3. ACCEPTING REAL-LIFE RUDENESS

58 **Duly Noted: Your Personal Protective Bubble.** See Elayne Savage, *Don't Take It Personally* (New York: Barnes & Noble, 1997), p. 163.

60 **Now mini stress-reduction sessions.** See the chapter "Red Light Means 'Relax'" in Richard Carlson's *Don't Get Scrooged* (San Francisco: HarperSanFrancisco, 2006), pp. 161–162.

66 **Duly Noted: Because We Let Them**. See Ginia Bellafante, "Can a Writer of Malaise Find Happiness in Acclaim?" http://www.nytimes.com/2005/10/30/fashion/sundaystyles/30Gaitskill.html.

4. HOW TO RESPOND TO RUDENESS

67 *Viva la Repartee.* Mardy Grothe, *Viva la Repartee* (New York: Collins, 2005).

68 A few years back. See "Rampant Rudeness: In the U.S. Today, 'Common Courtesy' as Contradictory Phrase," *Wall Street Journal* (Eastern Edition), March 12, 1987, p. 1. From ProQuest.

76 Estimates suggest that 25 to 30 percent. The results of the important study by Sarah Tracy, Jen Alberts, and Pamela Lutgen-Sandvik are in Sharon Keeler, "Study Calls Out Workplace Bullies," http://www.asu.edu/news/stories/200612/20061215 _workplacebullies.htm.

76 Gary Namie. Gary Namie and Ruth Namie, *The Bully at Work* (Naperville, Ill.: Sourcebooks, 2000).

79 Each month about 280,000 students. See "The Social Consequences of Being the Victim of a Bully," http://www.byparents -forparents.com/bullyingvictims.html.

79 800,000 miss school. See the 2003 U.S. Department of Justice School Crime and Safety Report.

79 In a 2007 survey. See "School Bullying Affects Majority of Elementary Students," http://www.sciencedaily.com/releases/2007/ 04/070412072345.html.

79 About 30 to 40 percent. See Kate McGreevy, "Cyber Bullying on the Rise Among U.S. Teens," http://www.heartland.org/Article .cfm?artId=18463.

79 Dan Olweus. See his book *Bullying at School* (Oxford: Blackwell, 1993), which I closely follow in this section.

5. The Near And Not So Dear: Spouses, Families, And Friends

101 **You're enjoying catching up.** The idea for this situation comes from Darcey Smart's "Advice Lady" column in the *National Post*, May 26, 2007, p. WP2.

7. Workplace Woes

112 **Almost 45 percent.** See the 2007 New Employment Law Alliance Poll, at http://www.employmentlawalliance.com/pdf/ELA%20Abusive%20Boss%20Charts031907.pdf.

112 **Many of us are logging.** See the ExecuNet study on the erasure of boundaries between work and life as reported by Brian Amble, in "No Escape from the Office," at http://www.management-issues.com/2006/12/8/research/no-escape-from-the-office.asp.

8. On the Road, in the Air, and Aboard the Train

126 **Risky incivilities.** See Louis Neipris, "Lifesaving Tips for Drivers," http://www.healthatoz.com/healthatoz/Atoz/common/standard/transform.jsp?requestURI=/healthatoz/Atoz/hl/sp/trvl/auto.jsp.

10. Digital Communication

155 **A Colleague Needs to Show More Respect to Your Staff.** The idea for this situation comes from James A. Martin, "Mind Your E-Mail Manners," http://www.pcworld.com/article/id,18579-page,3-c,tipstroubleshooting/article.html.

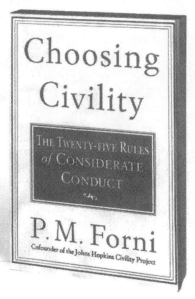